Until Death Don't Us Part

A spiritually inspired guide
to bereavement

Until Death Don't Us Part

A spiritually inspired guide to bereavement

Deborah Kay Hayward M.A

BOOKS

Winchester, UK
Washington, USA

First published by O-Books, 2010
O-Books is an imprint of John Hunt Publishing Ltd., The Bothy, Deershot Lodge, Park Lane, Ropley, Hants, SO24 0BE, UK
office1@o-books.net
www.o-books.com

For distributor details and how to order please visit the 'Ordering' section on our website.

ISBN: 978 1 84694 371 3

A CIP catalogue record for this book is available from the British Library.

Design: Tom Davies

Printed in the UK by CPI Antony Rowe
Printed in the USA by Offset Paperback Mfrs, Inc

CONTENTS

Foreword

By Minister Val Williams
International medium and tutor.

It was my privilege to do a private sitting for Deborah - one of those synchronistic times- the slot allocated for her sitting was actually for someone else. However, the Spirit world had other ideas.

Deborah's husband was obviously waiting to have a chat - sometimes I believe these messages are the telephone call home - a natural thing for a loved one to do so they can say they have arrived safely, usually when a journey has been made here on earth, but also when death has separated people.

Having met Deborah, been her tutor at the Arthur Findlay College and witnessed her dedication to promoting the truth of the fact that the spirit of her husband is continuing a progressive journey, I realized how much she will be able to help people, not only with her mediumship, but through her empathetic knowledge of how a desperately bereaved person truly feels. Mediumship is a means to emotional closure, a way of helping bereaved people to let go of the grief, and a great help in remembering the good times, memories which are often brought by the loved ones in the world of Spirit.

Spirit contact does not, as is often claimed, cause the vulnerable to be preyed upon - rather the reverse - the vulnerable can be given great help, and support when they KNOW that the love they shared has survived.

I am sure Deborah Hayward will bring a great insight to all who read her book - her husband must be very proud of her.

Minister Val Williams.

Introduction:
Why write a book on bereavement?

Every author has to ask themselves one very fundamental question: why am I writing this book? After all, thousands of titles are launched every week and few bring any real commercial success to the writer or indeed to the publisher. Yet sometimes we are drawn to do something because we simply *know* we must. An inner voice or our higher selves, intuition or inspiration refuses to be ignored and we know that the book must be born. In this particular instance, I decided to write this book in the hopes that it would help others to survive the ordeal of bereavement, and to fill what I perceived as a gap in the literature on the subject.

In November 2006 I became a widow at the age of 43, and my experience of this from a spiritual perspective, inspired me to write something, which might help others.

An avid reader of self-help books, I read every title I could find on bereavement, grief and loss to try and come to terms with what was happening to me and to my four school-aged children.

With very few exceptions, none of the books I read seemed to help.

The overwhelming problem with these books was their focus on 'letting go' of the deceased and admitting that they were dead and gone forever. A kind of 'wake up and smell the coffee: they're dead, get on with it,' approach.

As a very spiritual person this idea brought only despair and devastation, and one book in particular left me feeling bereft and suicidal.

In that moment I knew for certain that I had to find a different answer. I needed to bring alternative advice and comfort and hope to all the other millions of people that pass through bereavement every day.

With seemingly angelic guidance I began to be awoken in the night and writing materials would almost fly towards me. Bleary eyed I began to write as if the pen were magically guided.

At first I berated this exhausting insomnia, which could only be relieved by writing, but I quickly came to realize that I was being given a gift. A book was being given to the world that would bring great joy and comfort to others and it was being channeled through me.

At last my loss began to make sense, perhaps by sharing what I had learned I could help to heal myself and others.

I dedicate this book to all those who love and who grieve and to all our loved ones in spirit who have put this book in our path for a reason.

I would like to take this opportunity to thank all the mediums that contributed to my healing and all the friends and family members who patiently guided me and stoically supported me through life's greatest challenge: learning to live on.

I have aimed to provide guidance appropriate to all the various stages of grieving and bereavement; from the raw early days and weeks, up until the time when we might feel strong enough to consider what comes next in our own lives. For this reason the early chapters tend to deal mostly with the early emotions and reactions, and the later chapters begin to consider how we might wish, when we are ready, to move on.

Hopefully you will recognize yourself in some of these chapters and if a particular chapter doesn't feel right to you yet, do not feel discouraged, there may come a day, a month or a year from now when that chapter will be more meaningful to you.

For example if you have lost a partner very recently, you will probably not be ready to read a chapter which suggests that you may one day love again, or how to cope with a new relationship. But hopefully one day, even if it is a year or more from now, you may appreciate the advice, which intends to lovingly guide you through the possibilities of this new experience.

When my husband spoke to me through the wonderful medium Val Williams, who was kind enough to write the foreword for this book, he specifically mentioned that he wanted me to meet someone and love again. He also said that as I had supported him through his own widowhood, in the early days of *our relationship,* I would now know how to manage a relationship in which one of the partners was still grieving. This message came through for me when nothing could be further from my mind, but it did help me to feel that when the time came I would have his blessing.

Because my own particular most recent experience was the loss of my husband, I have focused mainly on dealing with the loss of a partner, but I hope that many of the ideas, concepts and suggestions will be equally relevant if your loss is of a parent or a close friend, a grandparent, an unborn baby or a precious child. Chapter 9 attempts to deal with the special grief that accompanies losing a child

People with an interest in evidence of life after death, paranormal experiences, or spiritualism may also enjoy the nature of this book, and I hope that counselors and friends of the bereaved will also find useful ideas and inspiration amongst the pages.

If you are presently in a relationship with someone who has been diagnosed with a terminal illness, you may also find comfort in the themes of the book, which aim to prove that death does not have to mean our parting, love is eternal. The personality, spirit and soul of every person lives on after the physical death of their body.

Great comfort can be had from this both for the living, the dying and the bereaved. Physical death is an adventure upon which we will all one day travel.

From the moment of our conception, our physical death at some point in the future is guaranteed, whether it be pre birth or in 105 years time. We will all part from our physical bodies, but the higher self; the holy, divine, spiritual essence of *Us* is source energy and cannot die. Like all energy it can neither be made nor destroyed it can only be changed, transformed and transferred. Whatever your beliefs about life after physical death or your point of view on the possibility of the existence of past lives or reincarnation, I hope that this book will help you gain faith or reinforce your present faith, that we do all live on. To not do so would be impossible.

The majority of world religions believe in an afterlife. This book does not aim to reflect any religious or political belief in particular, and its aim is to be broadly nondenominational. I personally cannot conceive of a God who does not love and value every person equally, or who believes that those who do not follow one strict belief system will not receive eternal life. I also believe that a truly spiritual person's personal belief system is continuously evolving and being refined, enlightened and adapted, as time takes them through the many challenges and experiences of life's rich journey. I believe this continuing development of spiritual understanding will even extend beyond a person's physical death. I do not choose to put my ever-evolving spiritual perspective forward as 'the truth'. The truth for each of us lies within us and is an ever changing and very beautiful part of our life's learning process.

You may choose to substitute during the reading of this book words such as God, our creator, universal energy, source energy, higher self, spirit, soul and any other words, which feel more meaningful and comfortable to you.

It is my deepest wish that every person who reads this book will gain some comfort and enlightenment, some inspiration and some strength. Above all this book is intended to be read with an open mind and to offer ideas and perspectives that you may choose to use or reject. Every part of your recovery is a matter of personal choice. On your journey you will meet those that believe in the continuance of life after life and those who, in the present moment, do not. The evidence for life in spirit is overwhelming and indisputable to those of us who have experienced spirit contact or who instinctively believe. To the non-believer it is often thought that no proof is possible.

I believe that we all have the innate ability to sense spirit contact, and to communicate with our loved ones well beyond their or our own physical death. If you are open to the ideas in this book, the chances are that you have already sensed, seen or heard contact from spirit, or that you *know* that one day you might. It is well known that we humans are typically using only a small fraction of our mental, spiritual and physical capacities. In truth it seems that we are afraid of our own potential and power as Marianne Williamson so eloquently writes:

> "Our greatest fear is not that we are inadequate,
> But that we are powerful beyond measure.
> It is our light, not our darkness that frightens us.
> We ask ourselves, who am I to be brilliant,
> Gorgeous, handsome, talented and fabulous?
> Actually who are you not to be?
> You are a child of God.
> Your playing small does not serve the world.
> There is nothing enlightening about shrinking
> So that other people won't feel insecure around you.
> We were born to manifest the glory of God within us.
> It is not just in some; it is in everyone.
> And, as we let our own light shine, we consciously give
> Other people permission to do the same.
> As we are liberated from our fear,
> Our presence automatically liberates others."

There are several distinct capacities that each person may have to a greater or lesser extent, which are involved in our potential to notice and understand spirit contact, and the messages of our guides and angels, or higher selves. Embrace and celebrate your abilities they are a gift. If you sometimes feel that you *see* the presence of spirit or guides or auras, you are blessed with clairvoyance or 'clear seeing'. If you sometimes just *know* or *feel* something like an instinctive certain knowledge, you are experiencing clairsentience or 'clear knowing', and if you *hear* spirit you have clairaudience or 'clear hearing'. During the grieving process you may feel that you do not care which senses you have, you are hurting too badly and all this may feel irrelevant. Or you may sooner or later decide to try to develop your communication skills with spirit and embrace all possibilities that make you feel happier and sure that we are not alone. Maybe this book will simply help you to have confidence in your own experiences from spirit. Sometimes people will dismiss genuine contact as 'imagination', 'hysteria' or 'wishful thinking' or they simply do not trust their own senses and perceptions because of the skepticism of others.

I am here to tell you that if you sense a spirit loved one near you, or think they are attempting to contact you in anyway; this is not your imagination. It is a sense that we have been encouraged to suppress and deny but which more and more people are embracing. We know that our departed loved ones are here with us, and I hope that the ideas in this book will help you explore and feel comfortable with, this wonderful blessing.

It is each person's personal choice and human right to believe what they wish to believe. Of course, you will make up your own mind about the nature of life after life, but I hope that you develop and affirm a belief in spirit, that will bring you comfort and strength every step of the way.

May loving angels and loved ones in spirit surround you as you read each page.

Please know that love is eternal and cannot die.

Peace and light

Deborah Hayward August 2009

Chapter 1.

'IT'S ALWAYS DARKEST BEFORE THE DAWN.'

My husband died of a brain tumor on November 16th 2006. That is an indisputable fact. However, everything that followed his physical death is open to interpretation.

Some of the phenomena which manifested to prove his continued existence in spirit may amaze and inspire you and will be revealed in chapter two.

Before I guide you to a spiritual understanding of grief and bereavement, and how a person can adjust to life after the death of a close loved one, I would like to share my own story with you. I am not sharing this because I like the sound of my own 'voice', nor because I think there is anything extraordinarily special about my experience, but to reassure you that just about every terrifying, numbing and bewildering reaction to death is 'normal' and okay. I am sharing this with you because I had a huge need to know that I was 'normal' during my early bereavement. Maybe this is true for you too.

I also want to show you the darkness that came before the light of healing and spiritual understanding, the darkness before the dawn.

I know that as time went on I wanted to find a book that would explain my journey in neat little stages titled such things as 'anger', 'shock', 'disbelief' and 'denial' and describe what to expect from each stage. Much like the detailed self-help handbooks I had read avidly during pregnancy, wanting to know every minute detail of what to expect during childbirth, I now wanted one to guide me through grief. I wanted to know it was okay to feel numb or surreal, or as though I was in a long bad dream and that any moment somebody would wake me up. I wanted to know it was all right to go crazy and throw all the washing up out of the kitchen window, or perfectly normal to feel like trashing my own home with a baseball bat. I wanted to feel that it was acceptable that even a spiritual person, who knew how to meditate and clear her chakras, could lose it occasionally.

I would like to tell you, in case nobody else will admit it to you, that all these things and more are a very normal and often necessary part of your adjustment to a new life. Even Psychics and mediums need to grieve. Val Williams covers this point very sensitively in her book 'Two Worlds as One: A Medium's Life.' By Red Wing Publishing 2001. No one is immune from grieving no matter how firm their belief in life after death, but a belief in the continuation of the human soul and the survival of human personality, can be a huge comfort both to the bereaved and the dying. I hope to impart that hope and faith in you during the pages of this book. Not every approach to bereavement is right for every person, we are all different and the wrong advice can have terrible consequences, as I will discuss later.

But for now, here is my story:

As a young woman of just 43 years old, living in Spain with four school-aged children, my life was suddenly turned upside down. My beloved husband Peter left his physical body and passed to spirit. He was dead. I have never felt so alone.

Minutes after his traumatic passing, a doctor began filling in the death certificate and a funeral director was filling in forms with me about what I wanted done with 'the body'. Moments later Peter's body was draped in a sheet and wheeled from the room. I was struck by how little this shell resembled my beautiful husband. I knew he was no longer attached in any way to the corpse that he had left behind. Yet I had strong feelings about how his body should be treated. Trivial things suddenly seemed very important. I was insistent with the funeral director, who had appeared like a vulture to retrieve its prey that the lovingly made gifts from our children that Peter clutched in his hands; should not be removed. Before I could think straight I was being driven across town to a Spanish funeral parlor to pick out a coffin and flowers and say how I wished him to be dressed and whether I wished his face to be shaved, my head was spinning and then I had to pay an enormous bill on the spot. Failure to do so would result in this vulture in a suit, turning up on my doorstep the following day to collect his debt. This thought horrified me. I felt like I was being swindled by the mafia. Had it not been for my dear father and his Barclaycard I do not know what I would have done, as I literally didn't have the money. It all seemed unreal, and we were told the cremation must take place by law within seventy-two hours, which meant that there was no time for friends and relatives to fly over from the UK. To complicate matters further there was no English-speaking cleric available to perform the ceremony and so we decided to do it ourselves.

The following three days and most of the nights were spent delving through a lifetime of photographs and choosing prayers and music to put together a DVD presentation for a ceremony fit to honor my brave warrior. We knew we would not be strong enough to stand up and speak at the front of a room filled with mourners and so we bravely recorded our readings and tributes to be played on the day. Several times during these three days Peter let his presence be felt in amazing ways, which I will describe in chapter two.

And so began my journey through grief and bereavement. A journey, which may know no end. I accept that. I cannot side step it or avoid it. It stares me in the face every day but through spiritual enlightenment and belief in spirit and life after death; my heart is steadily healing and so can yours.

My own financial situation meant that in the midst of my grief, I suddenly had to look for employment after a six-year career break, or we would all starve. There was no life insurance, just bills looming as far in to the future as I could see. Within one month of my husband's death, and still reeling from it all, I found myself working full time as a teacher in a British international school. Looking back I do not know how I did it, but I had promised my husband that I would be strong and take care of the children and I was determined to do so.

Despite the huge effort not to cry all day and to drag myself out of bed in the mornings, going back to work was a good move for me. It worked for me on two important levels; firstly the immediate financial crisis was temporarily abated and secondly I was insanely busy which kept me from having time to think. Unfortunately getting up at six in the morning to do the cooking and cleaning before work and then working without a break until ten in the evening, soon took its toll on the family and on my health. The children had just lost their father and now it seemed that I was too busy to be there for them either. I regret this but I really was trying to do what seemed right at the time. We need to be gentle on ourselves when we are grieving. Do not be tempted to think you are making mistakes, there is no magic answer, just do your best each day and take one day at a time. At first I thought my children were coping with my new regime and that we were doing stunningly well but in reality it was slowly all falling apart.

Each child suffered in its own very different way and this emerged through illness, and anger. Looking at it from their point of view they had gone from having two parents at home 24/7 to neither of us being there. It was tough on all of us. My children's personalities seemed to have changed; they were so angry and aggressive that I did not recognize them and I was faced with hatred and hostility every evening. I began to dread coming home from work.

When colleagues berated their working conditions, I had to admit that work was the only part of my life that was going well. I was glad to be there, away from the home and all the fighting and away from the memories that drenched the air in every room of the house. Away from the empty space at the table and the empty place on the sofa and the misery of a half empty bed.

My youngest child would eventually suffer a nervous breakdown, at which point I would have to take stock of what I was trying to achieve by working without rest or respite. At this point I would finally realize that I would have to give up my job.

Back to square one?

No, not really.

During the time that I was working I had journeyed through many stages of grief and had learned many lessons about life for the living, after the death of a loved one. These reflections and lessons are the subject of this book, which I hope will comfort and guide others that face a similar spiritual journey.

After the initial shock, numbness and relief that Peter's grizzly illness, suffering and death were over; came the many processes and challenges of grief. Keeping busy had been key to helping me cope with this, or more precisely helped me avoid dealing with it all head on. This time in my life was so overwhelmingly difficult to cope with. Living in Spain I was so far from my extended family that I was emotionally isolated. My best friend Angelines had died the year before and my other closest friends had chosen now to fall out with me over some triviality. My husband had been at my side for so long during life that I was used to him being my rock and the one to comfort me and now he was 'gone'. Without my man at my side, I felt that even after a busy day at work, reading a book might help me. Maybe some self-help grief and bereavement books would put me on the right path. As I said earlier, I longed for something to reassure me that everything I was feeling and journeying through was 'normal'.

There was no time for shopping and so I went online and a week later a huge parcel arrived from Amazon, filled with books on bereavement and grieving.

Some of these books were devoured in one sitting but as I slipped them back onto the bookshelf I realized with sunken heart that he was 'Still dead'. One particularly harmful book suggested that being strong for others and keeping busy were two very bad ideas. Socially instilled wisdoms they said, that would distract us from the real job in hand which, was to face up to reality and let go of everything to do with our 'deceased loved one'.

Okay, so suddenly the two things that were keeping me going were wrong.

Trusting this advice I followed their instructions about writing letters to the 'deceased' and talking about all unfinished business between us and forgiving everything and worst of all, finally writing him a letter saying a goodbye. This final letter left me absolutely devastated.

I cannot describe the devastation and desolation that I felt deep inside. It was like killing him with my bare hands and going through the loss all over again.

Everything I believed in, about life after death, was being taken away from me and leaving me with nothing but emptiness.

Convinced that I did not have to be strong for others, or to keep busy, I felt like giving up. Suicide seemed like the easy way out of my pain. 'Admitting' that my husband was not only dead but also gone forever was extremely detrimental to my mental health and spiritual well being.

Pretty soon, the conviction that my children no longer loved or needed me, made suicide an ever-present temptation. I could not face a world without my darling man; a world in which a life could be snuffed out and then miraculously 'forgotten'.

Thankfully one of my newest friends Jo, whom I now believe was guided to me by angels, was a natural born counselor. She had been through a similar journey following the physical death of her fifteen-year-old stepson, a few years earlier. Thanks to this wonderful friend I came to see that despite appearances, my children really did still need me.

They had become so angry and hostile lately that I did not recognize them anymore. My previously sweet little princess was telling me to "Fuck off" and "shut the fuck up!"

My previously very loving teenage sons would do anything rather than spend time with me,

"Just go to bed Mum it doesn't help us that you keep saying you miss Dad."

I felt unwelcome and unloved in my own home. I was working so hard to keep us together financially that every other area of our lives together had fallen apart.

We had been such a close and loving family and now the house was like a war zone, untidy in the extreme and fighting breaking out all over the place. All respect for me as a parent seemed to have gone and I really began to believe that they would be better off without me.

I guess it was scary for them hearing me wail like a banshee for hours on end every weekend whilst clutching an urn of their father's ashes. I guess I wasn't that easy to live with, but at the time all I could see was their hostility and disobedience, and their seeming lack of sympathy. They appeared happier when I was at work, although they had begun bunking school by now and I really felt out of control.

I would spend hours talking to Jo on the phone in the evenings and when she realized that the advice I had followed from the latest book had left me feeling suicidal, she became very concerned. Ultimately it was not my children that held me back from taking the easy way out but Jo's words. She became quite stern and told me frankly that if I did kill myself there was no guarantee that I would be reunited with my husband spirit side. A sobering thought.

When I finally linked the reading of this book with how I was feeling, I destroyed the book and the letters and tried to start my life over again.

I realized that it was time to seek medical help. A desperate visit to the doctor had me taking a low level anti depressant (fluoxetine), and this I believe saved my life. It helped me claw myself back from the edge and begin to cope.

Days and whole weekends spent howling like a wild animal in pain came to an end. Frightening sessions in which I literally felt my husband's soul being ripped apart from mine, abated. I learned to let go of needing everything to be tidy and controlled. Of course the advice books that I had read had all strongly advised against medication, a great plan if you can manage it. But if you begin to feel suicidal thoughts for goodness sake tell your doctor and get some help. One death in the family is more than enough.

I deeply regret having followed the advice of a self-help book, which ran contrary to my belief in spirit and the afterlife. I would strongly recommend you to avoid any book, which denies the continuance of life after death or that asks you to do any 'exercise', which makes you feel uncomfortable. At the very least regard all such 'therapies' with caution. If you wish to draw a line under your relationship with your loved one when they have passed and tie it up neatly and move on, maybe that advice is for you. But if like me you have received the feeling or belief that their love and spirit lives on, or have received contact from them in the form of flashing lights, perfumes or the sensation of them brushing your cheeks or other happenings that cannot be explained away by logic, please don't feel you have to follow expert advice that runs against your heart.

Letters of goodbye may feel right for some situations, but was very wrong for me. Now I would like to write a very different letter to my husband and I am so sorry for the goodbye letter that broke my heart.

Now I would prefer to write a letter of thanks, a letter of acknowledgement of all the love we shared in life and still share together in our new adventure, now that he is spirit side. I would like to write a letter telling him how he made me feel every time he kissed me or held my hand and how my heart skips at the thought of him still and always shall. It would not be a letter of goodbye or even of 'see you later', but more a letter of one heart speaking to another. A letter thanking him for walking by me now and always, telling him that I still notice his arms about me and recognize the signs and messages he leaves for us all.

And whilst I am in the mood for writing such a letter I could pen one to my dear friend Angelines who passed to spirit suddenly and unexpectedly in 2005 and remind her that we always said we would be friends forever and that her death hasn't changed a thing. I still hear her laughter and feel her merriment when I play the music we both loved to dance to. I would thank her for all the great times we laughed and cried together, for her love and for everything her friendship meant to me in life and means to me still.

And when I have finished that letter I could write one to my dear Nan telling her how much I love her and thanking her for the helpful way she literally throws things in my path at just the right moment, such as the perfect necklace to wear or the book I need to read.

Or I could write a loving note to my two baby girls spirit side telling them how much mummy loves them.

But the truth is that we don't need to write these letters. Spirit knows how we feel and what we are thinking. A thought or words said out loud can communicate our love, frustration, anger, disappointment, sadness or joy to them whenever we like. By all means write it down but thinking, singing and saying are all just as powerful to spirit.

Meanwhile, with the help of Jo's sensible and understanding advice and a low level of anti depressants coursing through my veins, I soldiered on in my grueling schedule. By now there was barely time or inclination to eat and my weight was dropping so rapidly that my clothes were literally falling off. Many new people in my life would never have guessed what I was going through, as I put such a brave face on things and I really was happy to be so busy at work, that there literally wasn't a moment to think about my own problems.

Unfortunately during this time, my children's need for me was going unrecognized. Pretty soon phone calls from their worried teachers would interrupt my class lessons and I would gradually find it was impossible to get them out of bed and in to school before I left for work in the mornings. All four of my children were regularly skipping school with mysterious ailments that I now know were all grief in disguise; the school year looked like being a failure. With hindsight (a fabulous thing), I wish I had taken them out of school for the year and just spent it as a family at home or traveling, but at the time normality seemed a commodity so precious that we just kept going.

When I did take new friends in to my confidence and tell them that my husband had died they looked so sympathetic. I told them I had been to hell and back, but deep down although I felt as though I *had been through hell*; I knew that I wasn't back yet.

Fortunately friends came into my life that helped me see more clearly, at a time when I had lost all perspective. I had focused on the immediate need to provide the family with money to buy food and pay the bills and was so determined to succeed at this at all costs that I lost sight of my true priorities. My children needed me at home, they were falling apart and I was just busying them along like nothing had happened.

Life had turned from a happy loving family situation in to a non-stop screaming match.

I found that I could cope all the time that somebody was around but the second I was alone, even in my car or in a lift, the loneliness would strike me through the heart and tears would come flooding back.

My youngest son's health was taking more of a downturn than I was capable of noticing. He was losing weight rapidly and literally seemed to be disappearing in front of our eyes. More and more stomach aches plagued his daily existence and nearly every morning would see a pantomime of him getting ready for school only to collapse in pain just before the school bus came and have to stay at home being cared for by an older sibling. Instead of staying with him I felt compelled by unsympathetic employers, to get in to work at all costs.

When I tried to explain my situation to my boss his attitude was I quote:

"It's not our fault that your husband died."

I really didn't know where to turn. I was reluctant to sell the family home, as it was something that my husband and I had built up together and a loving project was evident in every room. I determined to make ends meet come what may.

Eventually I had a friend come to stay when she found herself temporarily without accommodation. She worked as a teacher at the same unsympathetic school and was horrified to see how I had been managing. I think she really was incredulous at the state of my home and the sheer volume of work that I had to do with cleaning the house, feeding and organizing the family and our three dogs, as well as a full time teaching post. She began to see what I had been trying to cope with and I think she was very concerned both for my health and that of the children.

Eventually my youngest son collapsed just as I was setting out to work and it was then that my friend intervened and brought me to my senses.

"Look" she said sternly, "You cannot go to work and leave this child collapsed on the floor, he is really ill. Don't you dare come to work; they will just have to manage without you."

Thank goodness for sensible friends as, by now I had lost all perspective on life and felt that I would lose my job if I didn't attend and that this would be the end of us all.

As it was, Edward needed to be admitted to hospital urgently. He was badly dehydrated and had lost six kilos (about 14 pounds); he looked like a skeleton and was shaking and virtually unconscious. I dare not imagine what would have happened if I hadn't come to my senses and realized that this time he really was ill.

During this time it became clear that he was suffering some form of nervous breakdown and I knew that keeping my job was going to be difficult if not impossible. Sure enough my employers reacted badly to my having time off to care for my son and terminated my employment. This was devastating at the time but in hindsight was the best thing they could possibly have done. No matter what the financial implications, my family needed me at home and that was that.

Happily the three-month summer holidays were then upon us and a healing, re-grouping and re-bonding time could take place within the family. With the pressure of work and school off, sanity returned to the household. Swearing abated, tantrums ceased and harmony re emerged. Edward was still in an awful state psychologically and emotionally as well as weak and thin physically. He couldn't bear me to be out of his sight and panicked at the least suggestion of separation even for a few minutes.

Looking back I wonder how I let things get so bad, and equally I wonder how we all coped. Apart from pure adrenalin and the survival instinct, I think it was my faith in spirit, which got me through this very trying time. From very early on I was lucky enough to have been given clear signs that Peter was still around us, which I will share with you in chapter two. I have spent this time letting you know how bad things were for us during the first year, despite our belief in life after death, so that you will understand that I am not some holier-than-thou advocator of a miracle 'cure' for bereavement.

Losing a loved one, a soul mate, a husband, a wife, a parent or a child is a torture.

The feeling of being ripped apart inside when the loss is very close to you is about as primeval a feeling as giving birth, the wailing noise that emanates from a soul in torment cannot be faked or described. The feeling of wanting to 'understand' and of pleading with God to let you understand, why your loved one has been taken is equally hard to convey to anyone who has not experienced it.

So how can we heal from all this? How can we cope and adjust to life now that our special somebody is 'gone'? Ask out to the universal energy, your God, the angels or whatever brings you the greatest strength and open your heart to hear the answers. Maybe your answers will be found through the pages of this book, I truly hope so. For me the path to peace came unexpectedly on angel wings.

When I first knew that my husband was terminally ill I asked out to God, the universal energy, spirit and anybody else that might be listening to send me guidance as to what I should do. I knew that as well as being widowed, I would soon be without an income and this practical need weighed on my mind.

"Sell your Psychic Readings," came the unexpected answer!

Surprised by the nature and clarity of this message I asked out again:

"How?"

"On ebay!" was the surprising response from spirit.

Well I felt this to be a ridiculous suggestion; surely you would not be able to buy or sell psychic readings on ebay but I followed their advice and lo and behold there were pages and pages of psychic readings available. I picked a psychic that I felt drawn to and purchased a reading to see how this worked. I accidentally selected an Angel card reading, which I had never heard of, and this changed my life.

The reading was fabulous and my interest in the cards led me to purchase a deck of my own. Pretty soon I felt drawn to all things angelic and read avidly everything I could lay my hands on, on the subject. I became a great fan of Doreen Virtue the Angel Expert and soon had purchased all her books, cds and different card decks.

I found I was a natural with the cards and pretty soon I was doing some fantastic psychic and mediumistic readings for people all over the world. The accuracy of my mediumship was a great gift to my husband and me, as we knew then that we would be able to stay in contact forever. This was probably the most healing thing that could have blessed us at that time; the gift of knowing death would never separate us and that he would always be able to communicate with me. Afternoons spent with him crying, would now be healed by my saying,

"You are not going anywhere are you?" and then we would laugh together.

We knew our love would sustain us even through this.

I don't wish to trivialize how hard it was for us to separate physically, my husband put up a fight to stay in this life until the bitter end, he even revived three times from no breath and no pulse. He was determined not to leave the children and me alone, but he could not stay. His time to cross to spirit had come. He had to let go of his physical body and be reborn in to spirit. Those last few hours together on earth were torturously painful on every level but filled with love and so akin to giving birth that it was incredible. I will talk more about that in chapter three when we look at death as the beginning of a new stage in our soul's existence rather than as an end to it.

For now I just want to say that if you recognize my chaotic struggle through grief, be comforted because now I feel so at peace. I have come so far on a spiritual journey and through mediumship and spiritual understanding, have been given so much proof of life after death that I can now cope with the physical loss of my husband.

Of course I miss him, but I know too that he is still beside me. I have been lucky enough to receive contact from my husband through many different mediums which all confirm my own belief that he lives on.

Less than a year since my husband's passing, I qualified as a Psychic Practitioner and began my own Psychic Practice. Life is looking good again. I am writing inspirational columns for a newspaper and helping others with my psychic readings and mediumship. It is very healing to heal and help others. You cannot give without receiving so much back. It is an important tribute to our loved ones to turn their death in to something positive, as we will see in the chapter on making it count.

My youngest son Edward is now coping much better since I began to work from home and he recently described beautifully what it feels like to have a loved one in spirit:

"So Daddy didn't really die did he Mum? He just went invisible."

I couldn't have put it better myself.

Chapter 2:

Hello From Heaven

It is true to say that all Mediums are psychic but not necessarily true that all Psychics are Mediums. However, the skills used in picking up on non-verbal communication seem to have a lot in common. As a child I was very telepathic and psychic and often amazed my mother. She still tells the story of how at two years old, I would toddle in to the wool shop or grocers store and order exactly what she wanted, without her ever having told me verbally. I was certain she had told me as clearly as though she had used spoken words but of course I was simply picking up her thoughts and relaying them exactly.

Much the same skill is used when a medium passes on a message from spirit. The medium acts like a channel on the radio or a telephone, simply conveying the information as it is sent. This is a skill, which can take some time to perfect. Often a message will come through which seems too ridiculous to be correct but having faith in what you receive is vital. Sometimes that will be the most important part of the message from spirit and will give the recipient (the sitter), the clearest evidence that the message truly is from their loved one in spirit. Having faith like this takes nerve and commitment and the medium has to suspend the fear of feeling foolish or getting it 'wrong'. One message I had came as a visual picture of a man wearing a Gorilla suit, but I have learned to pass on exactly what I am given. If you don't pass on such a seemingly obscure piece of information the whole validity of what you have said may seem less tangible.

For example, once I had a long message from a lady named Dawn who showed me various cities and places and gave me various messages to pass on and kept showing me a parrot. For some reason the parrot seemed ridiculous to me at that time and totally out of synch with all the other images I had been shown, such as a suit of armor and a beautiful cathedral. However, at her insistence I passed on the entire message including the parrot and was surprised to hear the recipient say that the whole message was so meaningful to her and meant so much. The one thing above all else, which had validated the authenticity of the message for her, was the parrot, as this had been a code word and private joke between them through all their lives together!

One of the first times that I realized that I was receiving direct communication from spirit, came when I was thirteen years old.

I was sitting in a history class listening to the teacher when suddenly, the much-loved British comedian, Sid James appeared in front of me. He stood there for a moment and said very clearly:

"I have to go," and simply vanished.

This seemed very odd to me especially as none of my class-mates nor the teacher seemed to have noticed him there. I was still feeling puzzled by this experience later that day, when I suddenly had the surprise of my life. On the evening news came the sad revelation that 'Carry On' Star, Sid James had passed away.

He had suffered a heart attack, it was 26 April 1976, the opening night of The Mating season at the Sunderland Empire theatre, and Sid died on stage. The announcer called for the curtain to close and requested a doctor, whilst the audience (unaware of what was happening) laughed, believing the events to be part of the show. He was 62.

This was the moment that I realized for the first time, that I was receiving information and communication that others simply were not getting. At the time I felt unnerved by my new realization that I was some sort of receiver for messages from the unknown. It was like an unwanted gift at that time, yet in a way it felt special too, as though I had a kind of oneness with all spirit.

Some years later came a second celebrity spirit experience. I was walking home from town when suddenly I was frozen to the spot. A voice from spirit told me in no uncertain terms, that something devastatingly awful had just happened to the film star Elizabeth Taylor. As a keen fan of cinema of the fifties, I found this very hard to believe, but it was given to me with such intensity that I just prayed to be wrong. Of course, that evening the news would again solve a mystery as it was announced that the 'love of her life', Richard Burton, had passed to spirit. I went cold. I was dumbstruck to have received such a clear message again about someone I did not know personally and mystified as to why I was being given this information. Shortly afterwards the reception of information became even more startling as I began to pick up the radio on my teeth! I had small dental wires fitted to train my teeth and every night as we three sisters tried to settle to sleep in our shared room, we would be kept awake by my teeth literally broadcasting the shipping forecast from the local radio station!

This tied in with my theory that I was picking up messages from certain wavelengths as a kind of very sensitive receiver. These days I read books, which describe the human mind as a huge transmitter and receiver of information, such as 'The Secret' by Rhonda Byrne by Beyond Words Publishing, but at that time I had no such knowledge. I must be part of a very receptive family because at around the same time period my dear cousin Angela picked up Radio Caroline during an electrocardiogram test at St Thomas' hospital, much to the amazement of the staff.

My younger brother Kenton has always seen and held conversations with our Granddad in spirit and we only discovered this when my mother went to remove an old rug from the end of his bed, at which time he protested:

"You can't take that! That is where Granddad Soldier stands at night."

This seemed to be a fact as ordinary to him as the fact that the sun would rise and set each day. Children see spirit so naturally and they do not question it. As we age through childhood and puberty we may begin to ask questions, or have our experiences negated by adults who might tell us that it's our imagination, or just plain silly. This is a great shame, as we are effectively being cut off from a huge part of our own power and ability, and a huge source of comfort and wisdom.

My sister Susan also remembers spirit contact during her childhood:

> "Safety is the first feeling I get when I think of my experiences with loved ones who have passed over. My earliest memory of such an experience was with my Granddad after he passed to spirit, when I was just four or five years old. He visited me often in the school playground and walked with me at break time (recess), it felt ordinary, normal and very safe, I knew he was watching over me and making sure that I was okay. I didn't talk about this at the time because it just felt so natural and normal that it didn't seem worth mentioning, especially as any mention of his name would have my mother in tears in those early years. Many years later, at a family dinner, my brother mentioned that he used to see Granddad's spirit in the

playground too at that time, yet neither of us had felt the need to tell anybody about it, because I guess we accepted it as normal!

As a teenager I continued to have intuitive experiences and realized the power of spirit to let us know when someone we love is in danger. One night as I lie in bed asleep I was awoken by a feeling that someone was with me, hovering beside and over me. This didn't unsettle me too much but I obviously wasn't paying sufficient attention to the presence as I then began to receive electric shock type sensations in my body as though I was being prodded. I realized that the presence was trying to urge me into action and that it was concerned about a member of my family. Patiently I went through all the names of the family, receiving a shock each time until I mentioned my Grandmother, Nan. At the mention of her name a feeling of peace occurred, followed by a feeling of bliss and calm as the spirit seemed to feel it had conveyed its concerns. I then fell into a wonderful deep sleep but first thing in the morning I raised the alarm by phoning my parents and asking if anything was wrong with Nan. They replied that they were due to go away on a weekend's vacation but had received the unsettling feeling that they shouldn't go and my brother had also phoned to express concern. Urged by his unease, my brother decided to visit my grandmother where he found that she had fallen in the night and was unable to move. She was becoming very distressed and dehydrated and was found just in time to prevent a tragedy. I believe that the spirit that warned us all so strongly was that of my Nan's daughter, my Aunt Janet who had passed some years before.

Years later my Nan passed and despite her being 90 years old, I had trouble accepting her passing, I think she would have battled on if she could. Once she was spirit side she came to me every night to tell me off for having an untidy house! I felt unsettled by these visits and would get up in the night to tidy and declutter until she left me in peace! Even to this day, years after her passing, if my house becomes untidy she will materialize a photo of herself miraculously on to my dressing table or bed even though these photographs are usually tucked neatly away. I find my Nan's vigil reassuring and amusing and sigh and think I better get on with beautifying my house!"

The experiences of my siblings were never discussed until years after our childhood, I wonder how much richer our contact might have been had we been more open to it. I feel it is important to bring children up understanding and accepting spirit as normal, comforting, protective and reassuring and try to make light of any fears that they might have.

During the years that I spent at university, my psychic intuition seemed to grow but I did not welcome my ability and I think I blocked it as hard as I could, in order not to feel strange or different. One of the most frightening experiences that happened during these years was when I received or 'channeled' some automatic writing during a rather uninteresting lecture. I believed I was doodling but when I looked down at my pad I had actually written that a friend of mine was dead. This felt uncomfortable but I tried to dismiss it. Unfortunately, a short time later, that friend did die tragically in a car accident.

By now I was most frustrated with my abilities as they only served to worry and upset me and were never precise enough with times and dates for me to prevent tragedy from happening, so I could not see their purpose. I was afraid and I continued locking out this type of communication whenever I could.

About a year afterwards I was sitting on a train having a long conversation with my other Granddad, I recall every detail of what he was wearing and the beautiful scenery as it whizzed past the window. It was only as I left the train and slammed the heavy door shut with a 'bang' that I remembered that he had died a year earlier! I had just had a long, two-way conversation with my deceased grandfather in a crowded train. I was amazed. This time it felt good. I was glad to have had that special time with my Granddad and to have been so unaware during that time, that he now lived spirit side. It was wonderful and I felt very blessed by that visit. Even so, I did wonder whether anyone else had seen him there, or whether they thought I was talking to the wall!

This was the first time I remember feeling good about the gift of spirit communication. I felt connected to a oneness with the whole of creation, past present and future and I was elated. I was only in my twenties by this time and I had no real concept of how this gift or ability was going to light up my life and be a source of comfort to others.

As life goes on, it is inevitable that we gradually say goodbye to more and more people in our lives, as they take their place spirit side. I believe that with each loved one that passes over, our link to spirit and the bridge between our two worlds becomes stronger. You may find that your abilities to communicate with spirit become heightened during special periods in your life such as during a pregnancy or when falling in love or when faced with bereavement. There are times when we simply are more tuned in and more open to noticing and receiving messages, and signs from spirit.

I am so fortunate that my psychic abilities and mediumship began to open and unfold most dramatically, when I most needed them. Firstly when I lost over a period of time two babies through miscarriage, I found it a great blessing that my deceased Granddad Soldier would often bring them to my bed for an early morning cuddle. This is bliss and I wouldn't want to miss out on these visits for the world. You too can feel this deep joy whenever you wish, simply close your eyes and relax deeply then ask your spirit loved ones to come to you, then sense them draw near. That moment of half sleepiness last thing at night or as you first awake can often open channels of communication with spirit as you pass into a very receptive relaxed state.

I recently lost my dear puppies Angel and Bruce. They were missing for about ten days but on around the seventh night I awoke to feel little Angel jump onto my bed, she scampered up and licked me on the face! When I opened my eyes, there in the darkness was Angel but in a beautiful glowing spirit form. I was both happy to see her and feel her, and sad to think that maybe this meant she had passed to spirit somehow. Unfortunately a few days later both dogs were discovered where they had drowned, in a nearby water deposit. We were deeply saddened by this terrible loss but, I was able to comfort my youngest child, by reminding him that Angel had been to visit me in spirit and that he could close his eyes and feel them close at anytime. He did this and it was a beautiful sight to see him cuddled up with two invisible dogs, smiling lovingly and experiencing peace.

It is a huge comfort to be able to continue loving relationships beyond the separation of physical death. In spirit we are all still together. Without this knowledge, the death of my husband in November 2006 would have been impossible to take. Luckily my mediumship skills were heightened during his illness and it came to comfort both of us, that he could see me getting clear evidential contact with spirit and amazing spirit connections for people, through my work as a psychic practitioner and medium. We knew then for certain that we would stay in touch with one another after death had torn us apart physically.

This thought, whilst it could not take away the heartbreak of knowing that we must part from one another physically and that our children were about to lose their Dad, did help heal the situation on many levels. I would urge anyone that has a loved one with a diagnosed terminal illness to offer them the knowledge that love is eternal and that the human soul, spirit and personality survive physical death. Mediums work hard to provide evidence of this to all that need it.

The experience of receiving such evidence has been so important in my life that I wanted to share it with others; especially you. If you open your heart and mind to the possibility of communication you will almost definitely receive a 'hello from heaven'.

In 2005 I was away on holiday when the terrible news came that my best friend and neighbor, Angelines, had died suddenly and unexpectedly. She had seemed so well a few days before that I could not believe it. I felt something was getting lost as Spanish was being translated into English but no. At just 45 she had passed to spirit after giving a dinner party. There was no warning and she left two daughters, the youngest of who was only twelve years old. Funerals in Spain take place very quickly after a death and I could not get to be home in time for the funeral. By the time I got back she was already cremated and in her urn. I was lead in to her bedroom by her very shocked husband Pedro and took her ashes down from the shelf and hugged her for one last time. I was struck by the beauty of her silver urn, which was wrapped in midnight blue velvet. She was almost as beautiful and glamorous in death as she had been in life. But still none of us could really comprehend or believe that she was gone. After some time I realized that the reason that we could not get the real feeling that she was gone forever, and couldn't 'get our heads around it', was that it wasn't true. She was still with us in every way except in the physical and pretty soon she began to make her presence known.

The first sign I had from Angelines came when I walked up my path after the emotional moment with her urn and looked at my orange trees, it was October and they were in green fruit. Spanish Oranges are usually ready to eat at about Christmas time and have blossom around April or May the following year. Angelines had always loved the orange blossom season and we had often taken evening walks along the orange groves to inhale the heady fragrance. As I looked at the Orange trees i said to my husband,

"When the Orange blossoms come next spring I will take some to her as she loved them so much."

The very next day I was staggered to see that one orange blossom had appeared on the tree, all by itself. Wow! I searched the extensive orange groves and it was the only blossom to be seen. I smiled to myself; spirit had given me a clear sign. I knew she was still around me.

The following weeks were filled with strange occurrences such as coming back from shopping to find beautiful natural bouquets of flowers lying at my gate. Gorgeous swirls of bougainvillea, jasmine and other colorful flowers that I could not identify. It was tempting to say they had arrived at our door by the wind but looking up and down the street, the flowers were nowhere else to be seen, so I thanked Angelines and went inside smiling.

A short time afterwards my parents were staying with us and as usual we spent the evening playing card games. Every time that my husband or my father shuffled the cards, the Ace of Hearts would literally fly out of the pack. The first time it happened we joked that Angelines was saying 'hello' as the card had such a large letter 'A' on it and we had always associated her with a red heart. What began feeling like a joke became quite phenomenal, as Ace after Ace literally flew out of the deck. We felt quite stunned and impressed and by the end of the evening Angelines had us in fits of laughter at her creative antics! Ever since that evening she began to show me her presence by attracting my attention to a large capital 'A.' This became a very comforting reassurance, especially when we were to find ourselves in a chemotherapy waiting room and looked up and saw a huge 'A' on the door. I remember how I sighed with relief to know that her support was at hand.

These days if I want to spend time with Angelines I put on some music and close my eyes and feel her dancing and laughing near me. At other times we smell her familiar cigarette smoke or her perfume will waft momentarily by. I know she works with me as a guide now, as often during my work as a medium and psychic practitioner, I will get a message through in Spanish or she will sing 'Angie' in my ear. I cannot tell you how much I treasure the time we had together on earth but I will always value her friendship in spirit too. Friends, like love, are forever.

With my best friend gone to Spirit, life seemed flatter than before and I missed her daily visits and laughter, but the greatest blow came when my husband became ill a few months later, and I felt that she had deserted me just when I needed her the most. Anger is a very powerful aspect of grieving and this can be directed almost anywhere. Sometimes we are angry with God, the Universe, the world, the cigarette industry, an assailant or the medical profession. More often we turn the anger inwards at ourselves for not somehow having saved our beloved or for things undone or unsaid in life. At other times we feel anger at the person who died. We feel deserted, cheated, or abandoned, often at a time when we may have needed that person more than ever before. When Angelines had died I had felt anger at the world but when my husband became seriously ill I felt anger towards her for leaving me. She had picked a fine time to leave me and I wasn't afraid to tell her so!

However, it is a blessing in life if you can find the positive in every situation and pretty soon I came to realize, that she could actually help us more from spirit than if she had still been in physical form. She could now stand by us day and night and follow us everywhere and when Peter's time came to cross to spirit she could welcome him and guide him there. Grief is selfish; we know it might be wrong to blame the dead but they did rather leave us in it! Do not worry if you experience emotions such as anger, rage, abandonment, regret, sadness, devastation, numbness or disbelief. Everything is normal everything is okay. If it feels too dark or too painful to deal with, seek help either from friends and family or through counseling or medical advice. You will get through this. The sooner you feel that your loved one is still by you in spirit, the sooner you will begin to heal. If you do not feel convinced that the signs you are given are real, try having trust and faith and be open to a whole new kind of communication and experience. Visiting a genuine medium can help but be sure to get someone through a recommendation if you can. I shall list a few that I personally recommend at the end of this book.

My husband Peter was a strong and powerful figure in life and has persisted to be a very strong and communicative personality in spirit. I would like to share with you, some of my personal experiences of contact from him since his physical death, my own personal 'hellos from heaven'.

The day that Peter died I had to return home from the funeral parlor to our four grief-stricken children. We had seventy-two hours to put a funeral service together and we all felt stunned. Luckily my parents had been with Peter and me whilst he passed to spirit and were able to remain with us for another two weeks before they would need to return home to England. It had been Peter's wish that his funeral ceremony should be conducted in English and we were determined to make it as personal and wonderful a tribute to his life as we could. My father and my eldest son Daniel worked tirelessly day and night to make a movie presentation DVD to be played on a screen at the ceremony, as we all felt too upset to stand up and do our readings in person. The first task seemed to be to collate a lifetimes worth of photographs into a pictorial tribute, which would be played with appropriate music. Boxes and boxes of old photographs lay at our feet when my second son Kingsley plucked a sealed envelope from one of the boxes.

"It has never been opened!" He exclaimed surprised and handed it to me.

On the envelope was an inscription:

"To be opened after your flying lesson."

Everyone looked mystified as to why this had never been opened and I had to admit that I was surprised that my husband had never been tempted to open it. I had purchased a flying lesson as a birthday present for my husband ten years earlier but due to bad weather the flight had never taken place, despite many re-schedulings. In the end it seemed that he wasn't meant to fly. I had never realized that he had not opened this envelope given to him on the day.

"Let's open it!" pleaded Kingsley insistently.

I shook my head, as far as I was concerned, if it had been sealed for ten years it should remain unopened forever. But Kingsley was adamant that he just had 'a feeling' that it was meant to be opened today and right now. This was its moment! Well Kingsley had never said anything like that before and so I felt little harm could come of him opening it. We all watched with baited breath and you could have cut the silence with a knife.

Opening it carefully, he pulled an RAF air force insignia sew on badge from the envelope. (This is two wings.) There was a card with it too, and Kingsley gingerly opened it to reveal this message:

"To Peter – now that you officially have your wings!"

"That's because he is an angel now!" we all chorused in amazement.

It seemed incredibly beautiful to us all and amazing that this envelope should be opened on the day of Peter's death when it had remained sealed for so many years. We felt in awe of the magnificence of such a lovely well-timed message. His friends had affectionately known my husband as wing commander because although he had been in the RAF he had never flown a plane! The wings emblem was placed in his coffin.

The next day Kingsley awoke equally convinced that he should follow another instinct, which was to go and buy an acoustic guitar. It had been Peter's final wish to buy Kingsley a guitar, although I hadn't mentioned this to him yet, he seemed to know it. I did not feel like going anywhere so soon after losing my husband but could see that strong unanswerable conviction in Kingsley's eyes and so I agreed to take him to the only music shop in town. Kingsley had wanted a particular guitar priced at sixty Euros and that was the money that I thought I had in my purse, more or less exactly, so off we went. When we arrived at the shop we were disappointed to find that the guitar he had set his heart on had been sold. Kingsley turned to leave when he noticed a yellow guitar on display, and to my surprise he liked it very much. Feeling doubtful I drew nearer to take a look at this guitar and noticed it had a brass butterfly laid in to the neck and as butterflies were very special to me, I felt this was a good omen. Then we looked at the price; it was more than double the price of the first guitar and much more than I was sure I had in my purse.

"It's nice Kingsley but I haven't got enough money on me." I told him.

"Yes you have!" he said as though he had x-ray eyes! "Count it."

To my amazement I did have enough money in the purse down to the very last cent and I took this as a strong sign that he should have it but I wanted to be sure he liked it before parting with so much money.

"If you can play it you can have it." I announced.

So reluctantly he agreed to test it out in the shop feeling very shy and it sounded fabulous. We bought the guitar even though I wasn't sure where the next cent was coming from. When we arrived home with the guitar we noticed a swing tag attached to it that we hadn't seen before, it said 'DAD dio', We could hardly believe it and then we saw something else we hadn't noticed written on the neck IM HR 'I'm here'! Wow we both agreed that we had definitely been given some heavenly guidance with our choice and this bought us both great comfort. Peter was with us.

My daughter Elizabeth who was just thirteen years old and

had always been daddy's princess wrote a lovely poem, which she placed by her dad's photograph for the ceremony.

"Don't cry for me
I am already there
Happy and comfortable
And you know I still care."

Kingsley made his fingers bleed and stayed up for the following two days and nights to teach himself a version of 'Redemption Song' by Bob Marley on his new guitar. Daniel video filmed him playing and this formed part of the funeral service, even though Kingsley had felt too devastated to attend in person.

Meanwhile we were all choosing poems and readings and music to be added, as Daniel and my father worked tirelessly to get the tribute together.

I am sure Peter was pleased with the result.

It had been encouraging and comforting to have signs so early on that he was still with us but there was more to come. Once my parents had returned to England and the children had returned to school, I found myself alone for the first time since Peter's death. A huge amount of paperwork relating to sorting out death certificates, insurance policies and bank details etc was amassing and I just couldn't seem to get to grips with it. Peter had for part of his life been a civil servant and was so organized that he had always taken care of all the financial affairs, filing and paperwork. I was lost and felt that if I ignored it all it might just go away.

It was getting towards lunchtime and I was in the kitchen preparing something for the children's return from school, when suddenly a black pen came flying through the doorway from the lounge, at about six feet high. Narrowly missing me, it landed at my feet. Naturally I thought one of the children had come home early and went to see which one it was. No one was there. I was alone.

"Okay Peter darling!" I exclaimed aloud, "You are as powerful in spirit as you always have been and I get the hint, you want me to get on with my paperwork!"

I laughed and then looked at the pen again; it was a beautiful writing pen that I had never seen before. It was nearly always impossible to find a decent pen in our house despite our being writers, a teacher and students, and one was far more likely to find a stubby old pencil or a blunt colored crayon than such a lovely pen as this one. I was impressed and the hint was duly taken. I now understand that this pen was what is referred to as an 'apport', which means something put there or moved by spirit. I will never forget the way it flew at me that day!

The importance of these stories is that they show how our loved ones can make themselves known to us from spirit if we are receptive to their messages. Whilst it is not recommended to start over-reading too much in to every single thing that happens, signs like this need to be acknowledged and given your attention. Let your loved one know that you have received their assurance that they are still around you. Do not be afraid to hear their hello from heaven. You are not going mad nor are you imagining it or seeing things, you have just joined the millions of others who know the comfort of communication after death. It is a blessing.

Peter continues to communicate with us and of course I speak with him every day but some of the most phenomenal evidence of his continued existence came not through my own mediumship and receptivity, but through other mediums.

I was particularly lucky to be able to spend a week on a course at The Arthur Findlay College in Stanstead England in 2007, where the excellent international Spiritualist Medium Val Williams, was giving a course to mediums from all over the world. During our week together there was a phenomenal exchange of mediumship readings during the classes. I had forewarned Peter that I would be attending the course and that if he wanted a chance to speak to me through a medium; this would be the perfect time.

Well it seems that he took me at my word because he spoke to me through seven different mediums, none of which had previously known that I was widowed. Ingeniously he communicated in a different guise each time, much to the amazement of all.

I was trying very hard not to give anything away about my personal circumstances so that any communication would be genuine and not influenced by my situation.

In one of the first exercises that we did as a group we sat in small circles to do Psychic readings for each other as opposed to Mediumship. Peter Hind-Fletcher a very talented medium sat at my left and read for me.

"I feel a huge amount of love coming towards you from spirit. I see you talking to this man and you are looking between two warrior statues, maybe Greek warriors? I also see two swans and he is showing me green pastures. He wants you to go to pastures new and move on with your life."

I thanked Peter Hind-Fletcher profusely then explained that I had lost my husband and that I had his ashes in an urn between two Viking warrior statues, and that I did indeed stand and talk to him there. I also understood the two swans, as they are a traditional symbol for soul mates as they mate for life.

However the information about my husband was still kept in this small circle.

Towards the end of the morning Karen Harris a very accurate medium felt my husband draw near.

"I have your husband here" She began, "He is showing me himself reaching up and picking an orange from a tree and orange groves. I see him sitting on the terrace with his feet up reading a paper and listening to classical music."

"Yes" I replied, "we have orange trees in our garden and we always used to joke that he never sat down even to read a paper. The last present I remember buying him was a complete set of Classic rock, classical orchestra playing modern tunes."

"Now he is showing me when he was very ill, it doesn't look like a hospital where he died. He came out of his body and stood behind you. You were lying on the bed. He couldn't understand how you could bear to stay and see him that way. He wanted to be out of that situation but he couldn't bear to leave you, he tried so hard not to go."

"Yes that's very true although it was the hospital actually," I explained "but he never accepted that he was in hospital, I couldn't make him understand that at all, he kept asking who those women were that kept coming in and when I said that they were nurses he became quite cross and told me to stop telling him that he was in hospital, he simply did not believe it. Also he had a beautiful homely room with a bed for me and sofa and television and so on, it really didn't look like hospital you are right. Coming out of his body would make sense too as he 'died' three times and revived three times before finally passing over. He certainly did struggle to stay with me. At 1 am he was 'given' an estimated hour to live judging by the morphine and the fact that he had lost 2 liters of blood but he actually survived another 9 hours. Even the doctor was in tears to see such a brave warrior fighting to stay alive."

I thanked Karen and was glad to be able to bring her father through for her during the week.

Later that day we were all taking turns to practice 'platform' mediumship where we had to present our mediumship from the platform. Another excellent medium Andrew de Vaal took his turn and began describing a man.

"I have this man with me; he is tall with broad shoulders and a small amount of gray or blonde hair just at the sides. There is something wrong with his gait, he is having trouble walking, and he is shuffling."

I watched in amazement as Andrew's body took on the exact form and gait of my husband and he shuffled forward just as my husband, a previously very athletic man, had done towards the end of his life due to the illness."

Andrew continued: "I think he is about 85 years old and he is showing me orange trees."

Val interrupted

"Can anybody take this description?"

I raised my hand nervously,

"I can apart from the age; it is my Husband."

There was a gasp from the audience.

"He certainly felt that old at the end, as his illness affected his gait."

Then Andrew began an incredible blow-by-blow description of our villa in Spain. He gave details that no one could possibly know or guess, he described the way that cars passed by in front below the level of our garden, the shape and depth of our arched entrance, the terraces, trees and everything.

"That's my house!" I exclaimed really certain now that it was Peter communicating.

"He loves you very much… his one regret is that he deliberately failed at his education, he is proud to see his son doing so well, he should go to University," Andrew continued.

Val interjected "What is his message? What has he come to say?"

Andrew listened hard to spirit and said very definitely:

"Don't worry about the baby; everything will be alright about the baby, so there is no point worrying about it. That's what he wants to say."

Well it was a good job that I was already seated as this was the last thing I expected to hear and was especially worrying as another medium; the wonderful Colin Fry had given me the same cryptic message in the previous April when bringing through communication from my late cousin Angela. Given that I cannot have any more children myself, my thoughts turned to my teenage sons and I prayed that they were behaving sensibly! I have to remember that both mediums said I shouldn't worry about the baby but even so....time will tell!

Andrew de Vaal had done a fabulous job of bringing my husband through with so much undeniably accurate evidence that I felt elated. But this was just the start of Peter taking every chance to communicate, as we mediums constantly upped the vibration and built one reading upon another, we could all feel spirit growing very strong. Of course we all had our turns at reading for one another and I was fortunate to be able to bring loved ones through for others, as well as receiving so much for myself.

It is important for the continuous flow of universal energy that we all learn to give and receive in equal amounts, for to refuse to receive help, gifts or love will impede or block the flow for everyone. Many of us are so good at giving that we forget to allow others the joy of giving. Never deny someone the joy of helping you, remember how good it feels to give.

During the evening we all got into pairs to read for one another. I was lucky to be paired with Tom Harrison who is an amazing medium with a fabulously down to earth style. I think he would make a fantastic television medium and could be to the world of celebrity mediumship, what Steve Irwin was to animal programming and conservation. Even so I was very surprised to hear that my husband was coming through yet again!

"I have your husband here and he wants you to know that he has his bike! I see him riding it, it is not a racer it has high handlebars. I want to say that it is a 'Harley Davidson'. He shows me that he rides up and down the street on it circling around you. It is red and very beautiful with chrome details and beautiful matching leather panniers on it. It has a huge passenger seat behind him and he wants you to know that no one else is allowed on it."

"Is it for me?"

"Yes. He says he has seen Alan. He is very happy and having a lovely time on his bike and looking after you."

I was overjoyed at this news and explained why it meant so much to me:

"You have made me so happy Tom, thank you so much for that. You just described the bike that he always wanted exactly, he even had his photo taken next to one once and always dreamed of owning it. I was going to buy him a look-alike Harley just before he became ill and then of course he was not allowed to drive. My heart sinks every time I go past the bike shop in town thinking how he missed his dream, and now I won't have to feel that way because I know he has it at last!"

It is hard to describe the joy I felt picturing my husband driving his new Harley Davidson and it made me realize how much it means to deliver a clear message to someone from their loved one in spirit.

The next day Karen Harris took the platform.

"I have a tall man here very well built and strong, he is showing me Norway and the Norwegian Fjords for some reason."

My heart lurched surely not Peter again! He was of proven Viking descent and I always called him my Viking and we joked about his ancestors sailing over from Norway. I held my breath waiting for somebody else's hand to go up, but no one moved. Karen continued:

"He is showing me a Viking, Olaf."

"It's my husband again!" I confessed, "He was known as 'the Viking' and played a Viking in a play on stage once!"

Everyone was amazed at the number of times and different ways Peter was finding of coming through!

"What is his message?" urged Val Williams our tutor.

"He is showing me a black bag, and he says it's time to sort out your black bags."

Of course I knew exactly what he meant by this as all my unsettled bills and outstanding paperwork were stuffed higgledy-piggledy into black briefcases awaiting my attention.

Also he had insisted on buying me a black bag on our last outing and he had put some emergency money into it for me. Food for thought and yet more evidence that he was still around me and knew perfectly well how disorganized I had become.

During the week I had longed to have a private sitting with Val Williams but she was fully booked, so I had to resign myself to this being impossible. However, due to a mix up, one of her clients was told to wait in the wrong place and it seemed as though she hadn't appeared for her appointment. Val was disappointed and came into the class looking for her or a replacement volunteer for the appointment.

"I'll take it!"

I said as quickly as I could and rushed out the door to have this miraculously vacant slot. Val is an incredibly accurate medium and half an hour in her company was like having Peter in the room with me, and I shall never be able to thank her enough for her kind sensitivity. Her face lit up as Peter came into contact with her and she looked as many women tended to in his company, overawed by his charm and charisma!

It was lovely to see her enjoying his presence and I would like to share our sitting with you here.

Val Williams:

"I have your husband here and I am getting the name Roger."

Deborah:

"Yes Roger is a very dear friend of ours and tried to save Peter with Chinese medicine, he is a much respected Chinese Medicine practitioner and did a lot to improve the quality of Peter's life".

Val:

"I don't see your husband as old and frail like Andrew described him at all, I see him as very fit and strong and tall and handsome, absolutely gorgeous"(smiling).

Deborah:

"That's right his illness affected his gait at the end and he went from very fit to seeming very old at the end. He was very handsome yes!"

Val:

"I see he is gorgeous and all the girls used to think of him like a film star. Was he very fond of his hair?"

Deborah:

"Yes I used to call him 'The Fonz' when he used to comb his hair as he would do it with such style and throw the comb in the air and catch it!"

Val:

"That's just how I am seeing him with a quiff! I see him flexing his muscles. Was he connected to boxing?"

Deborah:

"Yes that's correct he was a boxing champion in the forces and used to weight train three times a week until his illness."

Val:

"Is there a connection with Jackie Pallo and Mick McManus; the famous wrestlers?"

Deborah:

"Yes that's right; Jackie Pallo lived near us when we met."

Val:

"Was Peter married when you met him?" asked Val looking puzzled.

Deborah:

"Well...Widowed yes."

Val:

"Yes he is showing me that there were three of you in the marriage and that you never made any fuss about his first wife's memory being kept alive. You understood and it was never an issue or a problem between you. He appreciated that. He wants you to know that there is no jealousy in spirit and even though he is with his first wife now, he still loves you very much. He always will. He says that although he did look at other women, as all men do, he never strayed he was always faithful to you. You were everything to him. When he used to hold your hand it was as though the whole world seemed like a beautiful place. He says 'you know; some people didn't understand our relationship, but we just used to make a joke about it.' We were very happy together. He says you are a beautiful woman, he always told you that you were a beautiful woman. He wants you to find love again now with someone else. But he says do not go out with somebody just for fun, that's no good to you, you need to find a man as good as me, a relationship as wonderful as ours, nothing less will do. Now I see him swaggering proudly and smiling as he tells me your relationship was complete in every aspect!" (Val blushes!)

Deborah:

"Yes it was."

Val:

"Don't go looking for a man on the Internet or anything like that he says, the right man will be 'put in front of you.' You don't have to look. He also says that you know how to build a relationship when one of you is widowed; you know how to do it. He would like to thank Andrew for the lovely way he delivered his message to you on stage. He admires Andrew very much and chose him, as he seemed to have the same depth of character and integrity as himself. He would like to thank Andrew for delivering his message exactly as he wanted him to. He says Carol too.

Deborah:

"Maybe that is Karen who also gave me a reading?"

Val:

"Maybe. He says you always knew that one-day you would be on your own and that he always tried to prepare you for that. But he also says that he used to really look after you and that in some ways he didn't do you any favors by protecting you so much. He hated the thought of you having to cope without him but now he says, as he is still with you all the time that you don't have to manage without him, he is with you…There is a lady spirit side who had a breast cancer but it was under her breast somehow and so didn't get detected until it was too late to operate. It couldn't be removed for some reason."

Deborah:

"Yes that's our friend Dawn."

Val:

"What a lovely lady she is ...Did you and your husband have a boy together?"

Deborah:

"Yes."

Val:

"He wants to say that nothing can compare with holding a baby in your hands, he is showing me hands not arms. He says there is a small trophy in the house, which means more than any other."

Deborah:

"Yes that is one we had specially made for our youngest son Edward"

Val:

"Do you have a grown up son?"

Deborah:

"He does from his first marriage."

Val:

"NO!!!! I don't think that's it, how old is he?"

Deborah:

"About 45."

Val;

"No, no, no, not him."

Deborah:

"We have a son who will be 18 this week, Daniel."

Val:

"That's the one, he is so proud of him. 'Please tell him he is the best thing that ever happened to me'. He sees he is struggling a bit at the moment with legal papers and responsibilities. He has a long way to go to be like me, he says, but he will get there, don't make him the man of the house it's not fair. Don't put so much pressure on him - he needs support. I can see him doing really well with his education and I am so proud. But support him more and take the pressure off him to be a man. It's too soon and no young boy should be looking after their Mum at his age."

Deborah:

"Thank you, that's good advice, I have been encouraging him to be the man of the house, its true and he doesn't like it. I will take the pressure off."

Val:

"Make sure you do as your husband is very insistent. Have you started your own little business recently, selling little things?"

Deborah.

"Yes, I sell crystals and angels and psychic card readings."

Val:

"He approves, it is perfect he says… he wants you to know that he loves you very much and that he wants you to be happy again with someone new."

Deborah:

"Thank you, that was wonderful, it, means so much to hear him speak through another person."

I coped well with this intense thirty minute sitting, which really *was* like half an hour in my husband's company, but fell apart later when a song was being played that I had chosen for the funeral; 'I had a dream' by Abba. It's funny how music sets you off sometimes and brings memories flooding back when you are off guard!

I have to say I felt better for a really good cry and bags and circles under my eyes seemed to disappear for a while. My roommate for the week Katherine remarked on it.

"I think they were unshed tears," she said.

As the week was drawing to a close by now I thought that

Val's wonderful reading would be my last contact through mediums for the time being but how wrong I was.

Just as the course was about to finish my husband grabbed the chance to come through again, this time through the lovely sensitive mediumship of Peter Hind-Fletcher.

"Deborah, I have someone here for you, he says Jack!"

I laughed

"That's my husband again he used to dress up as Captain Jack Sparrow! It was a private joke between us!"

Peter laughed,

"He is sending you a lot of love and he wants you to move on and be happy now with someone new. He is showing me the word Genesis, is that a reference to the bible?"

"No it was one of his favorite pop groups!"

"Aha, he shows me a tall strong tree symbolically; he shows me the green pastures again."

"Yes that's where we lived in England I think."

"He wants you to be strong like the tree; he shows me you moving straight ahead now like an arrow and going from strength to strength. He is very proud of what you are doing. But he says he knows more now than you will ever know!"

Peter continued to give me a very personal and sensitive long message from my husband which, I will not repeat here but suffice to say that he certainly made the most of his opportunities to contact me that week and give me a very strong succession of `hellos from heaven.´

No matter how many times I feel that I have assembled all the material I need for this chapter on spirit communication that I have received, Peter will surprise me with yet another way of communicating.

I can't end this section without telling you of the amazing experience my daughter and I had this weekend when she discovered Electronic Voice Phenomenon had somehow been recorded on her Dictaphone.

'Proof Paranormal' define Electronic voice phenomenon (EVP) as in essence:

'The capturing of disembodied voices via audio recording devices.'

More information can be found on their website www.proofparanormal.com. Many skeptics in the scientific community dismiss this phenomenon as explainable or over active imaginations or even downright fraud. However if this happens to you, you will be almost certain to believe it is genuine, especially when you have witnessed that no fraud could be possible. 'Proof Paranormal' explain that in *their* experience the voices:

"Answer questions, make comments about their surroundings and join in the conversation quite often! Some might say it all just sounds that way by chance, but statistically speaking well…not a chance!!! Also note the average comment like this not surprisingly often comes from individuals who have heard little or no EVPs at all. It is believed by many that the way in which a spirit achieves this communication is by somehow interrupting the electromagnetic field. Whatever means by which this communication is achieved, one thing is clear, the frequency at which it is done cannot be picked up by the human ear, but the recording devices seem to hear nothing short of what we call the dead."

You can probably imagine our surprise when my daughter had been recording herself singing only to find a strange unexplained ghostly voice appeared on the tape. She showed it to me and I agreed that it was odd and so we decided to record over it as it upset her. The re-recording however turned out to be more bizarre than the first. The batteries in the machine slowed down the play back and we could clearly hear the words 'I Love you' firstly in my voice (even though I had said nothing of the kind) and then the same three words repeated as if in answer, in my husband's deep voice. My daughter was petrified by this phenomenon but I explained that it was just another way that her dad could say hello. Had the batteries not 'malfunctioned' and played the tape back slower than normal we might have missed it. So I would like to say thank you to spirit for making that 'possible'.

Trying this at home with special equipment might seem to some as taking the communication effort too far, but for those interested in the so called 'paranormal' it is certainly very interesting and for me it was very comforting too.

Okay, so we have seen how many ingenious ways spirit have of making contact from blossoming flowers out of season, through making things appear (apports) and even imprinting their voices on to recording devices. Often too they will make a long lost or never seen photograph 'appear' at just the right moment, or arrange for a special song to be played on the radio at just the right time. Or they might stroke your hair, tickle your ears, whisper to you or place their arms about you. They can make noises in the environment and change temperatures and will stop at nothing to catch your attention. Can you imagine how you will be when you reach the world of spirit and try to catch a loved one's attention? Which method of communication will you choose?

Imagine yourself for a moment, invisible, weightless, free, filled with love and joy.

Now picture your grieving loved ones who feel you have slipped away from this world forever. Can you imagine how you might wave and shout to try and make yourself heard?

"Ooh yoo-hoo, I'm fine, I'm standing right here besides you; can't you see me?"

Maybe when you are ignored you will become frustrated and try making contact in some other way. Maybe you try wafting familiar scents such as perfume, aftershave, cigarette smoke anything to convey your continued presence.

Maybe you will point your loved ones at a book on angels and then make sure they chance upon a white feather when they least expect it? Maybe you will get really inventive and place flowers at their door, knock out light bulbs, or play your favorite tune on the radio at just the right moment?

Maybe you will stroke their faces in the night, tuck them into bed or whisper faintly in their ear? Maybe you can materialize momentarily in the chair, or flash an image of yourself in the mirror?

The point is this: you will find a way and all you really need is to have your loved ones receptive to seeing, hearing and feeling your presence.

If you have lost a loved one, be receptive to the signs. Notice changes in temperature, strange flashes of light, a feeling of warmth around your shoulders, or sounds, sights and fragrances that you associated with them in this life.

If you are blessed with the ability to believe and to still your mind you may even hear them speak to you.

I am sure many of you have a story to tell on this subject. I am sharing my story with you so that you will realize how beautiful, normal and reassuring relationships with loved ones in spirit can be.

Sometimes you will seek communication and at other times it will surprise you when you least expect it.

About six months after my husband's death I attended an evening of Flamenco starring the famous Spanish artiste Lolita Flores. The show was fantastic and I was enjoying it enormously when suddenly the friend at my side began to cry.

"What's the matter?" I asked her, seeing the tears streaming down her face.

"I have Peter here" she said.

I was taken aback as I hadn't expected that answer at all.

"He's really enjoying the show and he says it's much better than the one you paid a fortune to see in Madrid!"

I had to laugh at this as we had passed a dismal evening at our first and last flamenco show together, as a very thin man danced to the tune of someone moaning like a cat in season. I shared this with my friend:

"Oh it was funny I remember saying that the dancer looked like Tom cruise with anorexia and Peter had me in stitches when he replied that he looked more like a stick insect with Saint Vitas dance!"

"I never met Peter", she continued still very moved, "but I can feel that he was a good man and loves you very much and he says that 'by the way your legs *are* as beautiful as Lolita's to me and always were'."

This added a beautiful extra dimension to our evening as it was as though he were there with us as surely as if he had been seated beside us.

Often when we are bereaved and missing our loved ones we will wish dearly that they could be with us at important occasions such as weddings and births and I think that there is plenty of 'evidence' to suggest that they are with us at these times and this often comes out during medium communication.

Whatever form spirit communication from your loved one might take, I hope that it will bring you comfort, joy and warmth. Keep your mind and heart open and they will do the rest.

Chapter 3

SEEING DEATH AS A BEGINNING NOT AN END

If you have been with a loved one as they pass over in to spirit, you will probably have noticed how quickly their physical body seems 'empty' and shell-like. The spirit, soul and very essence of the person you love has vanished from sight.

So how can we explain this?

For thousands of years philosophers, religious teachers and scientists have tried to define 'the soul' and debated whether there is an 'afterlife' and if so in what form. Pouring over historical research and through religious theories can leave you feeling more confused and less knowledgeable on the subject by the minute.

In 1907 'Dr.' Duncan MacDougall actually sought to prove the soul's existence in a series of experiments in which he weighed patients close to death and then immediately afterwards. He claimed that the bodies lost 21 grams (close to an ounce), in weight. He therefore surmised that the soul weighed 21 grams and that the soul had a mass. Other scientists have largely discredited this research and there are obvious worrying ethical concerns involved in his experiments.

However no scientist, philosopher or religious theorist has ever been able to *disprove* the existence of the soul.

As a child I thought that the world was made up of spiritual energy. This energy gave life to people, animals, plants and trees. There was a finite and exact amount of this energy in our world all the time, just as there is a finite and exact amount of water. Water circulates through rain, rivers and evaporation to begin its life cycle all over again and I believed that spiritual life energy was the same. It would be impossible for your spirit energy to die, as it would sooner or later be needed to give life back into other parts of the living planet. No new energy could be made from a non-existent place so this made sense to me then.

As I became older and attended Grammar school, I was introduced to the world of physics which would remain a total mystery to me. Despite being the top student in many subjects including Biology, I consistently scored very low exam results in Physics. Teachers became cross with my 22% test scores and thought I was pretending not to understand or failing on purpose. They could not seem to comprehend that a seemingly bright student simply did not understand. Meanwhile I enjoyed long vigorous debates during our religious education classes, where I was performing at average levels. The reason I mention this is because thirty years later I was to have a rather unusual experience. I was sitting in a circle of mediums when Andrew de Vaal began to describe my school physics teacher in extreme detail, I listened incredulously and thought to myself 'this sounds like Mr. Oris, if he mentions his Concorde-shaped nose I'll know that it's him..'. Andrew stood up to show how lanky this spirit had been in life and how his suits had never been long enough in the arms or legs and how he had the most incredible nose.

"That's my physics teacher!" I blurted, amazed.

"Okay well he wants to bring you a message that says that you were more involved with his wife than with him weren't you?"

"Yes, that's right she was my Religion teacher and he was the school Physics teacher but didn't actually take my class very often."

"Well they have both come to say hello to you and are pleased to see you here."

"I didn't even know they had passed but I suppose they have done," I replied.

Andrew looked a bit mystified as he thought deeply and tried to blend with their energy.

"I am not sure what their message is for you...or why they came," he admitted.

In that moment I realized the importance of this loving married couple coming through to me. I had just begun a degree that would eventually make me a Dr of Metaphysics, which would be the blend of religion and science that their marriage symbolized. All those years before their interests had seemed so incompatible to me and suddenly it all made sense. It was great to know that they were still following the progress of their pupils and had made time to speak to me.

When it comes to a belief in the afterlife, science and religions still cannot agree. It is hard for the human mind to accept that things exist that they cannot see or feel with their five basic senses. Yet we freely accept that love exists, as well as hatred, jealousy and fear. We do not have to understand the mechanics of cell phones or satellites or TV to use and enjoy them. Some things we have to agree to accept and use without understanding them. Some things are beyond our true understanding. But that does not make them any less real. Think how hard it is to see the wind, we can see its affects on sand and leaves and the rustling of trees but the wind itself is invisible.

This book aims to give you a spiritual guide to coping with bereavement and not a scientific or philosophical debate. I am inviting you to open your heart and mind and take a leap of faith. After all as St Augustine said:

> "To the non-believer no proof is possible and to the believer no proof is necessary."

I ask only that you be open to the possibility that as we pass from the physical body we are reborn into spirit. Our personality, life essence and soul are preserved and continue to exist as the body is left behind. Think of it like a beautiful butterfly breaking free from its chrysalis.

These days technology gives us the means via special cameras, to show what some humans have perceived for centuries but not been able to prove: the existence of the human aura. We are beings of light and special photographic methods can reveal this. I was fortunate enough to have a sitting with aura photographers and aura readers, Angela and Nigel from Auraworld.com. I was fascinated to see my own aura, which ranged from red through orange to gold and its interpretation by Angela was amazingly accurate. You can find more about their work at www.auraworld.com. I asked them whether the aura leaves the body at death and they confirmed this, a dead body would show no aura in fact some aura readers can predict the imminent death of a person if their aura is absent, as they feel it leaves the body just prior to death.

Sometimes when you are in the presence of a person that you have never met before you can pick up certain feelings about them or sense an aura of goodness (or evil) emanating from them. Sometimes the power of their presence is so strong that we would have to describe them as having charisma, an energetic and radiating presence. Or maybe we find ourselves describing somebody as vivacious. There is simply so much spiritual energy radiating from within that we can feel it. It can be a pleasure just to be in the company of such a person and if we are meant to connect with them we will surely 'know' it. Similarly when we meet somebody and fall in love the attraction can be instantaneous as though fate has taken a hand and one or both of you will just 'know' that you are meant to be together. Or perhaps you will meet somebody that becomes an instant friend because you feel as though you have known each other 'before' as though you have been together in a former life. You will feel instantly comfortable with these people and you will often find that a series of seemingly bizarre coincidences have brought you together. Many people who believe in reincarnation of the soul believe that groups of souls are reincarnated together and that this explains our familiarity with some of the people who come in to our lives.

An example of this strange phenomena happened to me in June 2008. I was suddenly inspired to look on the Internet to see if there was a Mind, Body and Spirit Fair in my area at which I could sell my Angel readings, mediumship sittings and crystals. Amazingly there was a fair scheduled in a few days time about an hour's journey from my home so I rang the organizer to see if there was a table available for me but unfortunately the fair was fully booked, I asked her to call me if there was a cancellation as I simply *knew* I was destined to attend this event. Sure enough a cancellation occurred and I found myself planning a trip to the fair in Benidorm Spain the very next day. We had missed the first day of the 3-day event but now had a table for the remaining two days. Meanwhile, unbeknown to me, another very spiritual lady, medium and tarot card expert had had a similar urge to book a table at the fair and had been given her table at the last minute due to another cancellation. She had worked the first day of the fair opposite a very noisy exhibit of comedy and asked the organizer to move her to a quieter position for the second and third days of the fair, as the noise made her readings impossible.

Had she not done so, we would never have met because we found ourselves on opposite exhibition tables. Due to a failure of advertising the fair was very poorly attended and it looked as though we were wasting our time, but on a brighter note we began to talk to one another. During the next two days I discovered that this special lady was Helen 'Henry' Hezzell a very talented medium, who I felt instantly comfortable with. Unusually, my son Kingsley decided to accompany me on the second day and he went off skating with a friend whilst my daughter and I sat at the table, ever optimistic that a customer might chance by. At the end of the fair Helen and I chatted and she mentioned that she had a bar in Benidorm called 'The Black Pearl' which had a pirate theme.

"That's funny," I said. "I have a great interest in the films of 'The Pirates of the Caribbean' and have huge oil paintings of the main character at home and have hosted a 'Pirates of the Caribbean' Party!" We both laughed at the coincidence, and then Kingsley arrived.

"This is my second son Kingsley; he is a budding tattoo artist."

"Well my husband, Steve has a tattoo parlor and is an award winning tattoo artist!" Helen exclaimed.

At this, Kingsley's eyes lit up and at we all headed to the bar to see the Pirates decor and to meet Steve. Kingsley and Steve felt instantly bonded just as had Helen and I. Over the first year of our friendship Helen and I had some incredible experiences and coincidence after coincidence occurred, until I began to have some past life regressions. During these vivid regressions I eventually discovered that we had been together in many lifetimes and that she had in one lifetime been my mother. How wonderful that we had found one another again. Steve has become like a second father or older brother to Kingsley who now works with him as a tattoo apprentice.

I mention this story to help you realize that it is possible that we *do reincarnate* with the same souls in several lifetimes and that we will be together with our loved ones always.

I had a glimpse of this when I took a psychic journey during my training to be a psychic practitioner and met my husband who appeared as a timeless being of past, present and future. A full account of my psychic journey as I recorded it immediately after the event appears below:

Having reached a relaxed almost trance like state I had the following experience recorded in the present tense as I experienced it.

My Psychic Journey.

I close my eyes and set out to walk along a happy path to who knows where and it is a beautiful sunny day and I feel safe and happy. Suddenly the path meanders into the beautiful grounds of a stately home or castle. The grass is so green and the hedges are tall and strong, a group of happy people are dancing on the lawn in medieval style. Somehow I am aware that there are eight of them all dancing to beautiful music, but that I can only interact with one. She is young, about twenty years old and she has the most fabulous long red wavy hair with flowers in it. She is wearing the kind of rich, green, velvet gown that inspired Henry VIII to compose 'Green sleeves' for Anne Boleyn and I am 'given' that this is their time period.

I speak to her without words and she tells me that my spirit guide Rachel, is waiting for me down in the sunken garden on the other side of the hedge.

I have met Rachel on previous psychic journeys and I am pleased that she is waiting for me. I continue down the gravel path and come to a flight of stairs that looks impossibly steep and leads to a sunken garden far from sight. A leap of faith is needed because the steps look too steep to use, but I have been told that I will be safe at all times on my journey so I continue.

The journey takes me towards a great purple-white light and

then I find myself on the lawn of a beautiful sunken garden that has a lake in its midst.

I see more dancers but this time from an even earlier period and I know that the lady sitting on a rock is Rachel my guide.

I am pleased to see her. I sense that she is wearing a purple dress with white bodice and sleeves but I am disappointed not to be able to see her face very well. I try to focus on her shoulder or on a point near her head as I have been taught to do, but still cannot see much detail. Again we speak without words; I know from past contact that she is a soothsayer from the time of Richard the Lion Heart. Now she tells me that she has something to show me and she gently takes my hand. I notice that her pretty white feet almost glide across the grass and she is wearing no shoes.

She walks me further along the path and we come to a glade which I can sense is filled with fairies and I am lucky enough to see them there almost imperceptibly, but very real. I am amazed and delighted and then I see two beautiful little girls in Victorian type cotton nightgowns, playing and skipping happily.

Before Rachel can tell me I just know that these are my two little girls Rose and Holly, which I miscarried years ago. They run and take my hands,

"Mummy, Mummy come and see" they shout happily and a hot tear rolls down my cheek and I am crying watching this journey.

I am surprised to be heartbrokenly moved by all this as I was told that I would be safe and I took that to mean happy too. But still I was pleased to have some time with my lovely daughters who I miss so much. Happily they drag me onwards and I see my husband who passed to spirit in November 2006. He is young now and as handsome as he was in his youth, although he was always handsome to me.

"Look Mummy; it's Daddy, he's been looking after us and playing with us."

I melt into my husband's arms and I am sobbing so much that it hurts more than when he actually passed. To be able to hold him and yet not be allowed to stay. I can't bear to leave him a second time.

I want to stay but I know I have to return to take care of our four living children and to live until it is 'my time'. This is like heaven and torture both together.

Rachel comes to take me back and tells me not to worry I can come and visit anytime and he will always be there.

This thought comforts me enough to let go but I am still crying.

"You said I would be safe!" I complained.

"You are safe" Rachel tells me "but you have earthly work to do before you can come to live in the garden".

As she leads me back up the path I feel my heart will break but then I am stopped by two ladies whom I helped speak to their families through my mediumship earlier today, and I know I am meant to go back to my room and what we call reality.

As I ascend the steps Rachel stays behind and I pass the dancers once more. This time I am able to see two more faces in the group and they resemble myself and my husband and I know then that we have been together in many lifetimes and that we always will meet again and I feel happy.

I wonder now how I am to come out of my trance and so I say to myself

"You are wide awake" and I am back in my room and I am crying."

I have included this just as I noted it directly after the event, it is unpolished and clumsy but I hope that it conveys how we can walk into spirit and spend time with loved ones before returning safely back 'home'. This was a journey and not intended as a regression to past lives but somehow I had glimpses of eternity in all directions of time and felt the comfort of knowing we would meet again and again throughout lifetimes past and future. Amazing.

If you feel drawn to look deeper into theories of reincarnation and past life regression I would recommend the work of Dr Brian Weiss who makes the following observation in his book `Messages from the Masters´.

"We go through many stages when we're here. We shed a baby body; go into a child's, from a child to an adult, an adult into old age. Why shouldn't we go one stage beyond and shed the adult body and go into a spiritual plain? That is what we do. We don't just stop growing; we continue to grow. When we get to the spiritual plain, we keep growing there too. We go through different stages of development. When we arrive we are burned out. We have to go through a renewal stage, a learning stage, and a stage of decision. We decide when we want to return, where, and for what reasons. Some choose not to come back. They choose to go on to another stage of development. And they stay in spirit form…some for longer than others before they return. It is all growth and learning …continuous growth. Our body is just a vehicle for us while we're here. It is our soul and our spirit that last forever."

The idea that we continue learning and developing after physical death, makes sense of some of the comments that my husband has made more than once through mediums, that he has learned more since he passed than I will ever know!

Similarly my friend Jo often dreamed or sensed that her stepson Josh was in a special, spiritual classroom learning and this image brought her comfort.

Dr Brian Weiss also puts forward the comforting idea that loved ones reincarnate together in many life times and he has illustrated his evidence for this idea, through documented past life regressions. He also states that when a child is lost to miscarriage or abortion, the soul remains unharmed and will often reincarnate as a subsequent child of the same parents. Having lost two babies to miscarriage I found this concept particularly comforting and it explains why I never felt whole again until the subsequent babies were born. When my fifth pregnancy ended in miscarriage but we didn't plan to have any more children, I never felt whole as a person, or at peace. When a few years later we found I was pregnant again I was overjoyed, and when Edward was born I felt that the family and my soul were completed. It had felt unsatisfying and there was a lack of emotional closure and healing up until then. It is very hard to leave the last experience of pregnancy in your child-bearing years as a loss.

As well as past life regressions, Near Death Experiences (NDE) give many pointers to life beyond that of the physical body. The reports of many people who have revived from clinical death have common themes. Many experience floating outside their physical body and observing the scene of their apparent death. Equally many report a series of lights or deceased relatives coming to welcome them in to the spirit plane.

The beautiful film 'Dragonfly' starring Kevin Costner, covers this theory very well and might well bring you comfort if you have the opportunity to watch it.

Along with research into past lives, theories of reincarnation, contact through spiritualist mediums and direct personal contact, you may simply *just know instinctively* that your loved ones and others, continue beyond their physical lives. As shall we all.

It is apparent in one of Dr Brian Weiss's documented past life regressions that some of us reincarnate many times with the same family members and have different issues to resolve and challenges to meet in each lifetime. One of Dr Weiss's patients regressed to a previous life in which her brother had been killed at a young age; she noted that her parents in that life time were the same as those of her current lifetime. Suddenly she understood why her mother had always lived in fear in this lifetime that her son would die, and she had resisted becoming too attached to him right from birth, to protect herself from what she felt was an inevitable tragedy. This experience spoke to my soul as I had the feeling one of my babies wasn't going to survive once he was born. I hardly dared hold him and sure enough he did need special care and has had many physical and psychological challenges in his lifetime. An account of his early days of life appears in the chapter on angels. As well as my own early terror that he would not survive, he has always had the presentiment that he would not live to be eighteen years old. He often said

"You know, and I know, that I will never be eighteen."

After reading Dr Weiss' work I hoped and prayed that this was just an ancient shared memory of a previous shared lifetime in which he suffered an early death and in which I was traumatized as his mother. As I read Dr Weiss there were just 26 days until Kingsley's eighteenth birthday and I have to admit that I was scared. Having realized that this might be a past life trauma, I let the terror go. Thinking about it later I realized that his life had been saved from near death, in his eighteenth year, at least twice. The most dramatic of which was when his brother Daniel revived him twice, whilst waiting for an ambulance. Without his quick actions our fears might have been realized. On 27th June 2009 Kingsley celebrated his eighteenth birthday. History does not have to repeat itself if we can heal from previous traumas and life's' lessons. So let go of fear and allow good things to happen this time round.

As we saw when I went on the psychic journey, I encountered my spirit guide, my husband and lost babies, and I was amazed to discover myself with my husband in previous historical periods. In that wonderful moment, I knew we had been together in many life times and possibly always would be reincarnated together.

In a similar regression I learned that I had been a healing

woman whose success and psychic prowess had been construed as witchcraft. I already knew that in some lifetime I had been burned at the stake for witchcraft, but in this regression, I saw that I had been hung drawn and quartered, a barbaric ritual of ancient times, in which victims were hung and then cut down to be further violated, by being opened up literally into quarters, to reveal the intestines etc.

After this gruesome regression it occurred to me that elements of my current incarnation were reflecting this experience. I had recently been operated on in such a way that my intestines would have been bared and was now awaiting a liver surgery. The two operations together with previous surgical scars would probably leave scars similar to the drawing and quartering of a previous lifetime. This time, my challenge is to survive the knife and continue healing and using my psychic powers and mediumship for the good of others, without being persecuted. During the regressions I had seen one of my sisters many times but couldn't feel what our relationship was at that time, until a recent regression to the time of my execution, revealed to me that she was my daughter in that lifetime. This makes sense to me because there is an eight year age gap between us and when she was very young much of her care was entrusted to me, whilst my parents were working and like many older sisters I was blessed and challenged with the role of being like a second mother to her. It was in this same regression that I noted that Helen 'Henry' Hezzell had once been my mother.

Looking at your own life's challenges or those of your loved ones here and in spirit, might help you to see life as a spiritual journey of learning and growth. You may even wish to find a qualified past life regressions therapist to help you understand the challenges that you have already faced and to get a feel of what it is you came here to learn this time.

A good starting point if this interests you is Dr Brian Weiss's book 'Messages from the Masters. ' Doreen Virtue also does a past life regression meditation CD if you wish to explore this yourself.

What feels right to you at a certain time is safe to explore. Listen to your inner wisdom and inner guidance, which will always point you in the right direction. It may be that at this stage in your grieving, the concepts of reincarnation and past lives do not appeal to you at all. Do not worry for it is true that when the student is ready the master will appear.

I had Dr Weiss' book on my shelf for two years before I opened it, and yet I read it on the perfect day. It was just what I needed to know next. Similarly on your healing journey the right books, films, and people will be constantly put in your path at the right times. Books may fly off the shelves at you or you may hear the same author recommended three times by different people. Notice this subtle guidance. Your spirit loved ones and your own inner guidance and knowingness, will ensure that everything that you need to understand will be revealed to you at the perfect time.

The surest way to get in touch with your inner guidance, your inner wisdom or your higher self is through frequent meditation.

There is no mystery to meditation and anyone can learn to do it anywhere. In the beginning it is best to start with a quiet place in which you will not be disturbed. Adjust your surroundings to be comfortable and ensure that the room is tranquil and not too brightly illuminated. If they are available to you, candles and incense and soft music can help set the relaxing atmosphere. Or you may choose a guided meditation CD of which I will recommend some at the end of this book and there are many more at your bookstore, health shop, spiritual center or online.

I will talk more about meditation in the chapter on self-healing.

For the moment it is comfort enough to know that your loved one has not gone but has miraculously 'transformed'. All the physical restrictions of the physical body no longer affect or limit them. All illness, suffering, anxiety and pain are a thing of the past and nothing can harm them now. They are in a blissful state that we can only imagine and they stand by us and with us every day. Call upon them and speak to them whenever you feel the need and they will comfort you with loving energy. Their life did not end at physical death but rather began again in a new form and in a new dimension that we can barely comprehend. They will have learned more since they arrived in spirit, than we will ever learn in a physical lifetime! There is a huge amount of learning to be done when we reach spirit side and I am sure we in turn, will be able to use it to guide and support our loved ones.

How do I know that life continues after death? Well for me I simply always knew it, but have also been blessed by so much 'proof'. For you it may be necessary to take a leap of faith to believe that your loved one is still nearby or you might sense already that your loved one has been by your side all this time. The chances are that if you have felt drawn to read this book that you are already at least open minded towards the idea of life after death.

Many people that I have spoken to mention experiencing a sort of spirit visit a few days after the death of their loved one. This does not seem to happen immediately but rather it seems as though the deceased needs a few days to organize their energies, before they bless us with this amazing experience. Often people describe feeling as I have done at each loss that the spirit of their loved one appears like a beautiful peaceful energy, floating above them as they lay in bed. An indescribable sensation of peace fills the air above you in the shape of a person hovering angel-like in the air. You become filled with tranquility and the certain knowledge that your loved one is at peace and wishes you to understand that they are unharmed and happy now. This experience can be both unnerving and comforting, but most people describe it as leaving them feeling convinced that their loved one is letting them know that all is well for them. Don't feel too disappointed if this didn't seem to happen to you when you were first bereaved, it maybe that you were too distraught or distracted to notice. Rest assured that if you open your heart and mind to your loved one in spirit they *will* make contact.

Your loved one has moved on but has not moved away. There is no need to draw a line under their existence and accept or pretend that they are gone forever. Unless of course, that is what you want to believe. It is more a case that they have gone ahead, for as sure as we were born we will all die and move to spirit some day. It can be a comfort to know that we will be together again in spirit and that our loved ones will help us across to the other side. I know that in the early days of grief I felt comforted by the certain knowledge that I too would die someday. It made surviving without the physical presence of my loved one seem a little more manageable; knowing that it would one day come to an end.

People seem to instinctively know that a spirit relative or loved one will greet them when they pass to spirit and this feeling has been confirmed by many who have had near death experiences, premonitions or have witnessed the death of others. When my husband was very near to death I sat by his bedside praying for peace and release for him. I then saw his first wife and his sister (both deceased), walk straight though the closed door of the room and come to take him.

"Come on darling," I told him, "Norma and Pearl are here for you, it's time to go."

But my husband refused, even though he was strongly sedated he shook his head vigorously in refusal and they left us. This was an indication of how strong his will to live and stay with us was; he was determined not to let go of life one minute sooner than necessary. It is often said that man cannot die without his own permission and in that moment I could see that this might well be true.

Since passing to spirit my husband has been able to communicate most strongly that he hasn't left me at all, but whilst he was in his physical body I suppose that he was never 100% convinced that he wouldn't be forced to leave. He has always supported and looked after me and still does so from spirit side. It is he who awoke me at 4 am every night and thrust writing materials towards me almost dragging me out of bed to write this book. It is he who keeps me going when all seems bleak and hopeless and he who brings good fortune and opportunities to me now. His life did not end at death. The possibilities for his existence only transformed into greater more magical and spiritual things. I feel he can now support his family with love and guidance and angelic interventions like never before. We had a good communication in life and continue to do so. When I needed a job urgently I found the perfect one the next day! When I needed a car he 'told' me that the right one would have the number 2222 on it and so that I knew when I finally found it, that he had helped me to choose.

People often tell of strange happenings occurring such as photographs materializing in strange places at just the right moment or even of photographs taken since the 'death' of their loved one that have the person clearly visible in it. Spirit finds many ingenious ways to let us know that death was not the end of their lives, but a continuance of life or a new beginning.

It can help to know that your loved one has not gone but has merely become less physical and more spiritual. All the love that ever was, still is. All the personality, soul and spirit that ever was, still is. Reach out with your own soul and you will feel them so close by.

Anyone who has been through the agonies and ecstasy of childbirth will know how painful life transitions can be. The moving of a baby from the safety of its mother's womb out into an uncertain world is traumatic, stressful and joyful all at once. It is perhaps nature's greatest miracle and yet conception is the beginning of the end of every physical life. We have to accept that. But it is only the beginning for the soul, which will live forever. After birth, as after death, come many conflicting emotions and varying amounts of support from others. A new mother may experience great joy at the birth of her long awaited child and yet a few days later may feel uncontrollably sad. Hormones, the huge shock of such a life change and physical tiredness all play a part. Bereavement can be similarly exhausting, but it helps to feel that our loved one has in some way been reborn into spirit, the next stage in their life's adventure.

Some people call it 'life after life', as opposed to life after death and I think that is very appropriate.

As time passes and you begin to adapt to life without their physical presence, your loved one may choose to protect and guide you in less obvious ways. They may choose to remain less obviously present, hoping that you will at last find your own way. There is no need to fear this or to feel abandoned, they will simply be stepping back a little to allow you to build a new life, as they continue to develop spirit side. They may give you space to make new relationships or to rediscover your own strength. Never doubt however that they are still lovingly enveloping you in their care. You can continue to talk to them and pray to them all your life, as often or as infrequently as feels right to you. Just as a loving parent gradually encourages their child to be more independent and to stand, walk and think alone, so our loved ones in spirit nurture us towards self-reliance. The loving parent never stops caring and is never far from its child's side, and no matter how many years elapse they will always be there with loving support. So it is with our spirit loved ones. They are there to give as much or as little support as we need and are ever adapting to our new capabilities.

Recently I have found it very comforting that my husband continues to protect our children. His loving presence was very obvious as we called upon him to support our youngest son as he learned to ride a bike, his loving arms steadied the bike and our son's nerves and he overcame his fears and mastered a skill that had eluded him for many years. After repeated unsuccessful attempts, I whispered to him that Daddy was holding him safely on his bike, with that he whizzed confidently off down the road, exhilarated that he had at last mastered bike riding forever.

Equally we asked him to be with our eldest son during his important University entrance exams and with our daughter during her end of year exams. They drew great comfort and confidence from knowing that their father would be with them, in a way that he never could have been during his physical life. I continue to see my husband's face in crowds or superimposed on another at a crucial moment. We continue to know that he is here for us.

Another way in, which your loved one may be able to show their presence to you, if you are open to it, is through a display of spirit lights. You are most likely to be blessed by a visit of this kind in a dark bedroom before you fall asleep. Do not be afraid that spirit will ever make you feel uncomfortable or show you things that you do not feel ready to see. Ask the angels to open your spiritual sight and your third eye chakra (between your two physical eyes); if you would like to see more and feel ready. I will discuss more about invoking the help of the angels in the chapter on angels.

I was blessed by a truly spectacular display of these lights in October 2007 when I stayed at The Arthur Findlay College in Stanstead London. I was there on a mediumship course and was fortunate enough to have a wonderful roommate, Katherine. Katherine and I had never met previously (at least not in this life time) but we felt instantly bonded which was great. Katherine is one of the few people who I have been privileged to meet whose spirit guide was so powerfully present that you could see her stood behind her. I instantly saw her guide a beautiful American Indian woman who seemed to have magical or healing powers associated with her, a medicine woman. I was amazed by this vision and mentioned it to her. She said many people had seen the guide and told her the same thing. An hour later we walked into the cafeteria and another instant friend Karen took one look at Katherine and said to me:

"Do you see what I see?" she could clearly see the Indian too.

Katherine and I were following different courses during the day but passed each night chatting in our room together. We were both able to impart great wisdoms to one another and she was a great support to me during that week. Our bond and the incredible history of the college which is a center for spiritualism, was to open us up to one of the most amazing experiences of our lives.

It was Katherine's deepest wish to 'see' spirit and she asked out for this each day. One very special night we were chatting when suddenly in the pitch darkness I saw a shower of lights like a shooting star or a meteor shower. At the same moment Katherine sat up in her bed and said:

"Did you see that?"

"Yes!" I replied, relieved to have had a witness to the amazing lights.

Little did we know that we were in for hours of such treats. Slowly but surely more lights entered the room and performed an amazing variety of actions. Some crossed the room as if in a straight line. Others made firework patterns others hovered and others changed colors. Katherine was convinced that she had seen an angel. At first we had become alarmed and had put the lights on and sat up in our beds. But after some nervous discussion, we had decided that this was what we were here for and that we should tell the spirits that we were not afraid and would be very pleased to see them.

This leap of faith seemed to give the spirits great encouragement and it seemed as if they were testing our nerve. As the hours passed the lights became more and more daring and spectacular. All through the experience Katherine and I continued to confirm to one another that we were indeed both witnessing the same things. Next the air became misty and filled with lights like tiny stars; a thick cloud-like substance lowered itself gradually from the ceiling to the floor enveloping us and then disappeared, leaving a new clearer atmosphere. I commented to Katherine that this felt like the 'lifting of the veil' to reveal something from beyond. After that, the lights began to play in front of a mirror and their colors became more varied and intense. As we continued to praise and encourage them, the lights seemed to dare to come nearer. First they reached the far end of our beds and hovered there a while. When we did not show signs of fear they came nearer still, until finally they were forming a huge ball of light energy in between our two beds, near enough to touch. I trembled in awe; we could barely believe our senses. This was the peak of their activity, an unforgettable night leaving us in no doubt of the huge amount of spiritual energy created by that place where so many spirits came to visit so many mediums and loved ones.

Well if we ever needed any proof that spirit lived and played on, we had received it that night in abundance. I was interested to hear another medium comment the next day, when he went to retire to his room for the night, that he supposed he would be treated to the usual light show before falling asleep. To him this was a nightly occurrence and I think this reflected the advanced and powerful gift of mediumship that he had. Now that my experience is deepening I see lights more and more frequently but I have never had any experience to equal that which we witnessed in room 211 that night.

Physical death as a developmental transition of the soul, rather than an end to its existence makes sense. Since everything in the universe is energy in vibration, the concept of the soul continuing in another form is not too difficult to imagine or to feel. A mother may sense the soul and life within her child long before it is born, and we may sense the continuance of spirit long after death.

Some Religions may teach that animals have no soul and therefore do not continue after death. In that school of thinking an animal ends at death, yet many pet owners continue to sense their animals in spirit form and so I would contest that belief.

Recently we lost a small sparrow to death but a few days later at the same moment two of us sensed his return for a few seconds. His smell was unmistakable and we both commented on it at the same moment. This has happened twice. So if a beloved animal of yours passes to spirit, your sense that he or she continues around you is not purely wishful thinking. Neither is it any sin in my view to hold such a belief.

The agonies and emotions of birth and death have many similarities and this is because each marks our launch into the next stage of our soul's development. Take strength from the knowledge that your loved ones are ever present and that we will all meet again.

Every day that passes is a day further away from the day that our loved one passed to spirit and a day nearer to rejoining them, for we are all walking the same road. We are all walking towards God, some have gone on ahead but they have only let us fall behind for a short while. Each person is walking at their own pace, some stopping to smell the flowers or to help a stranger, and though we may choose different paths, we all have the same destination. We will all be together again at journey's end; reunited, jubilant and happy.

`A Course in Miracles' tries to teach us this:

In lesson 155, 12-14 it says

"We walk to God. Pause and reflect on this. Could any way be holier, or more deserving of your effort, of your love and of your full intent? What way could give you more than everything, or offer less and still content the holy Son of God? We walk to God. The truth that walks before us now is one with Him, and leads us to where He has always been. What way but this could be a path that you would choose instead?

Your feet are safely set upon the road that leads the world to God. Look not to ways that seem to lead you elsewhere...His trust has made your pathway certain and your goal secure. You will not fail... (God) asks that you think of Him a while each day, that he may speak to you and tell you of His Love, reminding you how great His trust; how limitless His Love. In your name and His own, which are the same...practice gladly with this thought today:

> I will step back and let Him lead the way,
> For I would walk along the road to Him."

I like the way this recognizes that we are all one with God, (however you may perceive Him or Her to be), we are all made with the same Divine spark within us and it is inevitable that we are and always shall be One Love. We walk together in a million different ways and take infinitely different paths and journeys but we all arrive at the same place. We are all going home to our Creator and will be with our loved ones both sides of the illusion of death.

We are all source energy and science agrees that energy can neither be made nor destroyed; it can only be moved and changed. James Ray explains this well in his contribution to Rhonda Byrnes' book `The Secret' published by Beyond Words, when he says:

> "Most people define themselves by this finite body, but you're not a finite body. Even under a microscope you're an energy field. What we know about energy is this: You go to a quantum physicist and you say, `what creates the world? ' And he or she will say, `energy. ' Well, describe energy.
> `OK, it can never be created or destroyed, it always was, always has been, everything that ever existed always exists,

it's moving into form, through form and out of form. ' You go to a theologian and ask the question, `What created the Universe? ' And he or she will say, `God. ' OK describe God. `Always was, and always has been, never can be created or destroyed, all that ever was, always will be, always moving into form, through form and out of form. ' You see, it's the same description, just different terminology.

So if you think you are this `meat suit' running around, think again. You're a spiritual being! You're an energy field, operating in a larger energy field."

This relates back to my childhood intuition that there is a constant and fixed amount of spiritual energy just as there is a constant amount of water being recycled again and again. My children often delight in telling me that we are drinking the same water that the dinosaurs swam in, although they put it less delicately!

It is important that we fully understand that our Divine spark, our soul energy, our spirit, and our personality cannot die. It is an enormous help to the grieving process if we realize that the very reason we cannot get our heads around the `fact' that our loved one has gone is because *they haven't!*

It is important that we learn to see the light in each person, their personality, their essence, because the rest is a temporary shell however beautiful it may be, the body is *not us;* we reside within it but for a short time. It is our vehicle for this journey on earth, it helps us walk our path but it does not come with us beyond the veil.

As G.K. Chesterton says:

"You must look into people as well as at them."

It is helpful if we can learn to see each other as light and love; part of one light and one love that unite us all.

`A Course in Miracles says in lesson 158:

> "Christ's vision has one law...It beholds a light beyond the body; an idea beyond what can be touched ...See no one as a body. Greet him as the Son of God that he is, acknowledging that he is one with you in holiness."

Maybe it is for this reason that it is so hard to represent what you love about somebody in a photograph. Often a friend I haven't seen for ages will ask for photographs of new people in my life but I always say:

> "You won't be able to see what is so wonderful about them in a photo, it is their energy and their aura that I love."

Certainly if your loved one passed with a terminal illness that left them looking very different to their earlier selves, you will not have loved them any less. My husband for example bloated, lost his hair and became unable to walk or talk, but he remained as beautiful to me as ever.

Although we may be able with some difficulty to imagine the demise and death of our own body, we can almost certainly not imagine the end of *our self* as a personality, if we have faith in eternal life. I find it hard to understand how anyone can see death as *the end,* I feel sorry for anyone who believes that this earthly life is all there is and that we are just `meat'. Those of us, who know we go on, are blessed.

I pray that you are blessed with faith in your hours of need and that you believe that your loved one's spirit still stands beside you.

Without my faith in eternal life I could not have handled the grieving process.

Faith may be challenged, but may it never leave you.

Remember this:

"Whom God has joined remain forever one."
A Course in Miracles.

There is no death for the soul, which has existed forever and will always exist. Past life regressions provide evidence of this. But whether you choose to believe in past lives and reincarnation or not, you will be able to feel and sense that your loved one lives on.

Chapter Four.

LOVE BEYOND THE VEIL

Continuing your relationships with deceased loved ones in a new way after the apparent separation caused by physical death.

When you lose a loved one you will find that you face several ways of dealing with your loss, all of which you may find yourself drawn to at some point. You can spend your time wailing, screaming like a banshee, smashing plates or clutching at precious articles of clothing, teddy bears or even an urn of ashes but sooner or later you will find that none of these things bring your loved one back in to your life. Alternatively you can go in to denial about the existence of life after physical death and try and reconcile yourself to the 'fact' that your loved one has simply ceased to exist and try to believe that they are gone forever. You might try subscribing to the belief that you have to 'come to terms' with your loss, or heed advice to 'pull yourself together and get on with life'. You may even begin to get the sneaking suspicion that others will become bored or embarrassed by your grief if it should seem to last too long in their eyes, or worse still that you offend others by feeling happy and do not appear to be grieving enough. You might feel you simply cannot win.

Few people will ever really know how much you hurt inside or how hard it is to adapt to a new life without that special someone's physical presence. Few will truly understand the depth and magnitude of your own personal loss and grief, just as they never truly understood how much you loved the person in their lifetime. Do not waste time wondering what others think of your behavior, if they are true friends they will stand by you, if they are not, be prepared to let them drift gently away.

If you have lost a partner, you may find it helpful to make new friends that never knew you as 'half of a couple'. You might find yourself struggling to remember who you are outside of that special relationship and new friends can help you to find your way back in to being a single person again. Don't worry if you find yourself buying extra food for someone who no longer needs such sustenance, or find yourself cooking for two, or making two cups of tea or coffee when only one is needed. I find it helpful to try and laugh at this now and make a joke with my husband in spirit. During the initial months of adjusting to life without his physical presence, it was often these moments that knocked me to my knees with grief revealing a chink in my armor of bravery. I well remember collapsing in a heap in the supermarket the first Christmas after Peter died when I stopped to buy six Christmas Santa hats and my daughter reminded me that we now only needed five. I had been coping with so much so stoically but this took my breath away. It is the unexpected moments that creep up on us and catch us unaware that often bring tears flooding back.

It is a useful aim to decide that when you find yourself reminiscing, or something brings memories flooding back, that you will look back and smile rather than look back and cry. Try to hold all the joy and happiness that was in your relationship, in your heart and mind, and choose to forget the more painful aspects. This doesn't mean we should deify our loved ones once they have passed to spirit and pretend they were perfect or that they never caused us pain. Rather it is a way of being gentle with yourself and supporting yourself as you adjust to the new you and the new way in which you can continue to relate to your deceased loved one.

Of course your loved one in spirit will be doing everything they can to support you and let you know that they are around. Whether they do this by leaving you signs, moving objects, whispering, playing your favorite tune on the radio or by impressing their presence upon you; if you are open to their communication you will soon realize that they are around. But how else can you continue your relationship? I find it comforting and helpful just to simply carry on speaking to the person in spirit as though they are still physically present. I can often be found chatting away to my husband when I am 'alone' in the car and will often either pour my heart out to him or simply joke about things that are going on in my life. In my third eye I can feel him sitting beside me there, guiding my journey and advising me, probably cringing at my driving as he always did! This type of contact can be as casual and frequent as feels natural to you. You can communicate equally well without the need to speak out loud; for spirit can pick up on our telepathic speech and thoughts just as well. Speaking to them in your mind will elicit just as much contact with your loved one now, as calling to them out loud.

People often refer to praying to their spirit loved ones just as they might pray to God, saints and angels. This is a similar communication given a different name. In some cultures the ancestors play a major role in religious and spiritual beliefs and this can be similarly reflected in the hearts of those who believe that their grandparents and parents stand by them in spirit. There is no need to feel foolish if you wish to carry on a full talking relationship with your loved ones in spirit. If you speak to others you will probably find at least one admitting to speaking to their deceased mother or grandparent, and yet more who will be willing to share their experiences of having felt that they have received communication from spirit. I was lucky enough to meet a lady who prefers to remain anonymous, at a Spirits in the Sun event in Spain who had always felt her grandfather's presence with her and I was delighted to see the photograph she had accidentally captured on her mobile phone which clearly showed her grandfather as spirit leaning over and kissing her forehead. There is a huge amount of paranormal research, findings, photographs and video evidence of the continuance of spirit after death but few things are as convincing to the individual, as their own personal experience of receiving communication from spirit side.

For different people different signs and communications will seem appropriate. A friend of mine, who lost her dear daughter at just five years old, always feels that her daughter is making contact when she seems to manifest rainbows at important and unlikely times. The rainbows are her way of knowing that Nikki is trying to say hello and that she is helping and still around the family. The sustaining comfort of this is enormous and I feel that none of us should try to explain away the conviction of another that they have received loving spiritual communication or advice.

Okay, so on a practical level how can you continue your relationship with a loved one, once they have passed to spirit? I began with a prayer to my husband telling him that I would always love him and miss him and asking him to wrap his angel wings about me and support me as I bring up our four children. Strictly speaking of course this wasn't the real beginning of our love and life together after the separation of death because we had been blessed with time to discuss it before he died. My mediumship and our joint belief in the power of love to last an eternity and survive even death, was very sustaining during the painful months in which we began to realize that our physical life together was coming to an end. For us preparation for our life together in spirit had a head start. We spoke about the fact that although his physical body would die, he would not be going away from us all. He would stay with us and guide and protect us. I promised faithfully to make a good job of raising our children and that I would be okay and survive. These were some of the hardest conversations we ever held of course, along with discussing his wishes to be cremated. Love can bear all and you will survive this. The will to live, even if it wanes during grief and bereavement, is very strong. Call upon your spirit loved one to lend you strength, courage and guidance. Ask them to stand by you now more than ever and do not be bullied by others into 'letting them go', so that they can move on with their own spiritual development before they are ready. They have all eternity to do this and now is a good time for you to be selfish and ask for help.

Others can help you to keep your relationship alive by allowing you to talk freely about your loved one, without always quickly changing the subject. All the time that a person is spoken about, remembered and loved, they truly live on.

I remember that when my dear friend Angelines passed to spirit her young daughter came around very distressed a few weeks later, telling me that some unkind child was repeatedly phoning her to say that her mother was in an urn in the lounge and that it was all very odd. I looked at this beautiful 12-year-old child and told her, your mother isn't in the ashes or in the urn, *you* know where she is. Look in the mirror and you will see she lives on in you, you are a part of her and she is a part of you and she lives on forever in your heart and mind. Even with my clumsy Spanish translation, the smile that filled her face told me that she knew that this was true.

Many people gain comfort from keeping favorite photographs on display as a way of connecting with the spirit of a loved one who has passed. A photograph can be a good focus point if you wish to lose yourself one more time in the eyes or delight at their physical appearance and recall the time you spent together. It helps some people to feel more comfortable speaking with spirit when they look at a photograph and can be more tangible than speaking to an invisible presence.

Of course holding a beloved item, which still carries their unique scent, can also evoke their presence in your heart and mind but if none of these items are available you can still call them into your heart and mind through quiet reflection or meditation.

If you wish to spend time together on a deeper level still it can be comforting to try a psychic and spiritual journey to meet your loved one. You can do this by consulting a Psychic Practitioner or by listening to a CD designed to guide you through this process. The best one I have discovered for this is Val Williams' CD `The Rose Garden´.

Time I spend with my husband when I take Val Williams guided CD journey, is beautiful and special and now that I know that I can repeat it whenever I need to, it feels less difficult to part from one another. I know that he will always be there.

I don't think we should worry that our attachment to spirit will somehow delay their own spiritual progress, as I am sure that life in spirit is so multidimensional that it is quite possible to achieve both enlightenment and to stand by our loved ones. Families for example often report more than one member having achieved communication from the same spirit person at the same moment, even though they were in different physical locations. I feel it is quite possible that when we are spirit side we will be able to simultaneously watch and comfort all of our living loved ones even if they live far apart from each other.

You do not need to be a medium to stay in contact with spirit. Any open-minded person can talk to spirit and become aware of spiritual guidance, presence and signs. It is helpful not to feel afraid or silly, and helpful if you can learn simple meditation techniques to heighten the contact possible with spirit, but really all you need is love and a willingness to communicate. Simply talk to them either aloud or in your mind as though they were still physically present and you will feel the comfort of knowing that your relationship didn't end at death, it just changed. Soon you will become aware of all the wonderful things that your loved one will now being organizing for you from spirit side. This could be new job opportunities, the perfect house, and a perfect new partner when the time comes along. You will find you are getting a heavenly helping hand. It pays to have contacts in 'high places!'

Other ways in which I keep my relationships alive is by talking freely about the loved ones in spirit without embarrassment and without tears. My children especially the youngest have come to readily accept spirit as part of their world having grown up with a mother who works as a medium and psychic.

Edward our youngest regularly 'sees' his father standing behind him in the mirror and speaks about him in the present tense. For example 'Dad says' rather than 'Dad used to say', which clearly shows that he knows his dad is still around.

You will find your own favorite ways of communicating, as will your loved ones. Some spirits will choose to communicate telepathically with you and others will make their presence felt by moving objects near you or by organizing amazing 'coincidences'. If you remain open and willing, you will know that they are there.

One lady recently wrote to me to express her sadness that a playful spirit loved one that she had acknowledged no longer seemed to be around her. I suggested that this person only wanted to let her know that he was fine and around her and that having acknowledged his presence he had lost the need to be so evident and was now just quietly around her. This felt right to her and she felt very comforted. Often our needs in grief can be largely met by gaining a positive perspective and focusing on love, eternity and open communication. You might find yourself throwing the book across the room at this point depending on where you are at with the grieving 'process'. I think it will certainly be worth re reading this book and any others you have found partially useful, from time to time as you gain new perspectives. Advice you receive in the early days can feel inadequate, trite and meaningless or may bring vital insight and relief. Usually spirit or angels will guide you to people or advice that will comfort you and later you will have the opportunity to support others in turn.

It can be useful to speak with others who have traveled through grief, to seek professional help or to visit a medium and most of all to call upon your loved one who has only slipped from view and will never be far from your side. Let them guide and support you now.

Chapter 5

POSITIVE STEPS TOWARDS SELF-HEALING

There are almost unlimited ways in which you can help yourself during the healing process, from changes you can make in your environment to calling upon the angels. It is good to keep your mind and heart open to the endless possibilities for feeling better and if you have a particularly bad day, remember that it is just that: a bad day: not a sign that all your healing work has failed.

The time has come to learn to love yourself. It can be difficult at times to remember that you are an important person and need to be the focus of your time and attention now. When you have lost a loved one it is a good idea to consider diverting all the love and healing energy that you used to lavish upon them during their physical lifetime, into looking after yourself now instead. This idea may seem alien to you at first, if all you feel like doing is lying down to die, or if you have put yourself at the bottom of a long list of priorities for many years. Many of us associate self-love with conceit or vanity, but that is not what I mean at all.

Probably we have grown up in an environment where we were encouraged to feel 'less than' or ugly or undeserving. Early religious experiences may have led us to believe that we were sinful or dirty or worthless. Sexism in the classroom may have led us to believe that intelligence was unattractive or boastful, or pointless. Years in a relationship may have led us to almost lose contact with our inner selves. We may feel that we have temporarily forgotten who we are. Perhaps we have become defined by our relationships to others, you may have introduced yourself for years as 'Edward's Mum', or 'Glynn's Daughter', or 'Peter's Wife.' Relentless bombardments from the advertising industry may have convinced you that you are overweight, or wrinkly or in desperate need of remodeling. Few things in our environment have deliberately set out to make us feel good about ourselves. It could be that falling in love with yourself now will be like getting to know a stranger.

So how can we begin to let down our defenses and learn to admit, even if only to ourselves, that we are a beautiful perfect child of God, a unique and special gift to life and someone worth nurturing?

Begin with self-care, rest, sleep, exercise and eat sensibly to the best of your ability. Maybe you are finding it difficult or impossible to eat properly, if at all. Sometimes it can feel painful or pointless to cook a meal for one person, if you have been used to cooking for the two of you. But you must take care of yourself; your loved one will be urging you to do this from spirit. Try not to neglect your nutritional health as skipping meals makes feeling better so much harder. Be gentle with yourself if you decide convenience foods are the way to survive just now, the point is to make sure that your body is getting enough fuel to cope with the stress of bereavement. You can go back to creating masterpieces in the kitchen when you feel better. Always take up offers of help and kindness if you can, but don't beat yourself up if you really would rather manage on your 'own'. Of course we are never truly alone, as we are surrounded by so much love in spirit. Other aspects of self care can be enjoyed as soon as you feel ready, such as pampering baths, quiet meditation, walks in nature and whatever brings you joy. (Yes joy: give yourself permission to be happy even if it is only a fleeting moment, enjoy and embrace the infinite possibilities of finding something to feel good about.)

If you feel you would like some guidance with learning to love yourself; the best author on the subject in my opinion, has to be Louise L Hay.

At some point in your journey you may feel ready to explore some 'letting go'. This does not refer to letting go of your loved ones continued presence, unless that is what you need, but rather letting go of accumulated emotional scars from childhood, adolescence and adulthood that may be holding back your healing process. Louise L Hays 'You can heal your life' and accompanying workbook are excellent ways of exploring this area. I wasn't drawn to this wonderful source of self-healing until two years after my husband's death. As they say 'When the pupil is ready the teacher will appear', and I think this is true of books, friends and inspirational messages and revelations. They always come to us when we are ready. Sometimes you may have a book on your shelf for many years and never have read it, but when you need that perfect message or idea you will be drawn to read it. Maybe just a few specific pages will fall open 'as if by accident'. I feel we are guided by spirit at these times to read or hear just what we need, just as I hope you felt guided to this book. Working my way through Louise L Hays books and cds has been extremely healing for me, even though it brought issues to the surface that caused me a lot of pain and the occasional healing crisis, I feel I know myself much better now. These books are an indispensable guide to 'loving the self' which so many of us find so difficult, and although they don't focus specifically on bereavement, I think you will find them a valuable addition to your healing resources.

The basics of loving the self include, acceptance of yourself as guilt free and worthy, and letting go of a lot of things from your early years which damaged or upset you and remain unforgiven, you may find yourself needing to let go of anger and unforgiveness surrounding the loss of your loved one too.

Another area you may wish to consider is creating a healing environment.

In the early days after bereavement it may take a huge effort to brush your hair and clean your teeth, let alone attempt anything as challenging as the housework or your usual chores. I can well remember standing looking at a pile of washing up thinking it represented a challenge equal to scaling Mount Everest. I can remember combing my hair one day before I went out (in the clothes I had slept in) and thinking I was making a special effort! Activities you used to take in your stride might seem overwhelming during the early stages of grief and it is very normal to find the house of a bereaved person looking as though a hurricane just blew through it, even a year or two after their loss. Chores pile up, paperwork seems impossible to face, the ordinary becomes extraordinarily difficult to achieve. But this will gradually improve with time so have faith and try not to despair if it all seems hopeless. Take comfort from the fact that this is perfectly normal. Meanwhile accept any practical help that is offered with open arms! At the other extreme are those of us who cope by getting everything super clean and tidy and organized in an attempt to feel that we are 'in control' of at least one area of our lives. If this is your reaction you will benefit from the good flow of energy around your home and a sense at least on the surface of some calm. However do be careful not to try to be superwoman or superman at this time, it is important not to exhaust yourself. Also you may wish to beware the over clinically clean and tidy look that might bring home the emptiness you may feel at times. Whatever feels right for you will make you most comfortable but be gentle with yourself either way.

I remember that in the first six months of my bereavement I

held the belief that if I could just get on top of the housework and get the place tidy, somehow everything would be all right. Finding my home in a mess every day when getting home from work made me feel as though my life was out of control and none of my four children seemed to be willing or able to help. I became quite obsessed with the idea that the main problem in my life was that my house was untidy and that my children were rude and unhelpful. Then came one of the biggest blows of all as I realized that, even if by some miracle a team of twenty cleaners were to appear, or a fairy were to wave a magic wand a make it all clean and shiny, my life was not going to be all right. My husband would still be dead. There was no bringing him back into physical being. This realization dealt me such a body blow that I literally just wanted to die. My need to be in control of some aspect of my life had focused on the housework something I felt physically and emotionally totally unable to do. Trying to explain this to tidy level headed friends was quite impossible. I felt like people despised me for living in a mess. Even my very good friend and neighbor came around at one point to blame me for an invasion of rats he was experiencing, a totally unjustified accusation but it was a humiliating experience having him inspect my house with disdain. I felt later that I should have said something clever like: `Not all of us can afford a cleaner', but at the time I was too shocked to offer anything except surprise and disbelief that I was being treated so thoughtlessly. Why, I wondered, didn't people offer help instead of criticism? I think the answer of course, is that almost no one on the planet has any real idea what you are going through inside. Maybe you are managing to present an image of coping with life when in fact your life has imploded and everything is too difficult to describe. Even I made judgments based on appearances when I deemed my children rude and unhelpful and lazy when in fact inside they were grief stricken, depressed and terrified.

With hindsight I now recognize that these feelings of panic

and despair associated with my untidy living space were a natural instinct trying to offer me a sanctuary of calm. It was some time later that a friend introduced me to the principles of Feng Shui, which made perfect sense of what I had been feeling. She explained that a clean uncluttered space allowed the flow of 'chi' or energy to move freely and bring peace, happiness, success and even prosperity. Eager to try anything that might help; I enthusiastically followed the principles and managed to tidy and free up a lot of positive energy within the house. This might be healing for you but don't feel disheartened if you don't feel up to it just yet, even small steps to follow the principles of Feng Shui might be healing for you. It is surprising how much grief can be intertwined with our living environment; especially if it is the home you once shared together during your loved one's physical life. I found that I simply couldn't sit in my living room at all because the sofa looked so empty without my husband sitting there. My Feng Shui friend walked into this room for the first time and said how depressing it was. She could sense that he had spent his last days there. The culprit she said was the icy blue painted walls and she recommended that I paint them 'Magnolia' which is another word for cream in my book. When I repeated this suggestion to my daughter I was amused to find her reaction mirrored my own: pure horror!

"Mum we can't possibly have it Mongolia that would be so boring!"

This caused an enormous laugh as I explained it wasn't Mongolia but Magnolia and we both vowed we would repaint the room, so that no one ever said it looked depressing again. The result was a very rebellious bright orange for the walls and a fuchsia pink ceiling! Needless to say my friend wasn't terribly impressed but the therapy of laughter, rebellion and joint physical exercise involved with the decorating, had been very therapeutic to my daughter and me. Also the living room lost some of its association of so many memories, which gradually induced me to spend short periods of time there again. Redecorating, clearing clutter and unused items and treating yourself to some new sofa throws or paintings for the wall, or bringing plants or a water feature into your living space, are all ways of lightening the atmosphere and raising your spirits, this can be as inexpensive or as lavish as your budget dictates. It can be healing to choose colors that your loved one may never have picked or go with something you always wanted but wasn't to their taste. This establishes the beginnings of a new period in your life in which your guiding light is now within you. Equally you may prefer to keep things just as they were and some people are adamant that nothing should be disturbed or discarded. If you feel this way now, keep your heart open to the idea that one day you may wish to make some changes, but do not allow others to bully you. Do what feels right for you. Grieving is a very personal process and we all recover and move towards our new lives in different ways and at different rates.

If you are caring for a bereaved person for goodness sake don't be fooled by surface appearances, inside the person is almost certainly trying to cope with a pain they have never experienced in their life and have no idea how to deal with.

One of the most healing things that you can do is to make time to meditate or spend quiet time by yourself. Soaking in a bath with candlelight and meditation music can be very healing especially if you choose a guided meditation CD. I will suggest some good ones later.

One exercise which I find particularly helpful is the one advocated by Doreen Virtue who has been instrumental in my work as a healer, angel worker and psychic, through her inspirational books, audio CDs, Angel cards and inspirational talks. You can find more about Doreen at www.angeltherapy.com. This exercise is called 'The Corral visualization' and features in her book 'Healing with the Angels.'

"After relaxing with several slow, deep breaths close your

eyes and get into a comfortable position.

Imagine that you are standing in a country field. A road is leading to you—one that brings all your material, emotional, and spiritual supplies. The road passes through a corral to get to you. The corral has two gates: one facing the road, and one facing you. If both gates are open, supplies readily flow to you, and your gifts to the world flow from you.

Whenever we hold unforgiveness towards someone, we imprison that person in our minds where we mentally flog them with our pronouncements of guilt and blame. The image of the person we resent is 'corralled' in our consciousness, and the gates to the corral slam shut like prison doors. You necessarily go into the corral along with the person you've judged in order to monitor their imprisonment. So, both gates are shut, and your locked corral blocks your flow and supply.

Look inside your corral right now and see who's there. See the high price you pay for corralling these people. If you are ready to forgive, imagine the gates of you corral automatically opening. Visualize whoever is in the corral walking out, free, happy and forgiven. Wish them well. If this seems difficult try forgiving the person instead of their deeds. As you forgive feel the release, the relief, and the renewed energy as your resentment lifts. Check that you are not in the corral alone out of an ego judgment you hold against yourself.

Recheck your corral often, especially when you feel tired, ill or afraid. You'll find that these are the times when you have the most people (including yourself) locked into your corral. Once you open the gates and clear the corral, your emotions and energy level will improve."

This very healing exercise can be performed anywhere at any time when you feel the stress levels rising. It is a good starting point for self-healing because unforgiveness towards yourself and others erodes your capacity for happiness. Do not be alarmed by who you find in your corral during this visualization. It is quite natural to find yourself and your deceased loved one in there. Maybe you secretly feel abandoned and betrayed by your loved one? Maybe irrational thoughts such as how selfish they were to die and leave you in this mess have found their way into your mind. Don't feel guilty about these thoughts. But do forgive your loved one for leaving and forgive yourself for feeling resentful. Maybe it is God that angers and disappoints you. Let it go. Maybe a thoughtless friend or relative, who said the wrong thing at the worst time, is in your corral. Free them now. Maybe the vultures that descended to argue over your loved one's estate have upset you. Maybe you hold anger towards medical professionals who failed in your eyes. Let them free. Perhaps you resent somebody for not having supported you more. Perhaps you are angry with yourself for not being stronger or for being powerless to prevent the death of somebody so special to you.

There will be many 'what ifs' and 'if only's' to be dealt with but it is vital to accept the fact that you could not have prevented your loved one from passing into spirit at their allotted time, any more than you can hold back the tide.

Let it all go, drop your shoulders, and shed any tears that still need to be cried. Scream if it helps, nobody will mind. Even if they do you will feel much better and one day they will understand.

Another good way to promote your self-healing is to address anger issues that may be bubbling beneath the surface. I found a Nintendo Wii Virtual boxing game found on Wii Sports, exceptionally therapeutic! When my children handed me the controls and I had to punch the air repeatedly and aggressively to knock down a virtual opponent, I felt fabulous as I knocked him over. Biff! As a pacifist I was surprised how much I enjoyed and needed this physical outlet for my anger and grief and I would recommend any such therapy to you so long as you are sure you will not harm yourself or others! I can barely believe I am advocating violence but I hope that you understand the type of outlet I mean. Wii Fit now has a boxing game in which you punch a punch bag for those of you who would rather keep it less violent! Arcade games where you have to punch monsters back into the ground when they pop up, a punch bag or a game of vigorous golf can all help vent that feeling that life is unfair. I also felt but did not try, that a stack of old plates lined up to be smashed by throwing a ball at them would be fun, just as we used to in the old fashioned fairgrounds. Health and safety though please everyone protect yourself from harm with goggles!

Okay so now you have let go of unforgiveness and let out some of your anger you might feel ready to benefit from other therapies and exercises that will help with your physical, spiritual and emotional healing. Do not forget that your loved one stands by you in spirit throughout your adjustment to your new life and relationship. I don't want to call this your 'recovery' or talk about 'getting over it' as I don't think this is what happens at all. It is more a case of adjusting to the fact that your loved one has slipped from sight and touch and is now around you in a different way. You can talk to them and sense them but you are learning to live without their physical presence. Often this feels so hard as perhaps they were the one person in life that helped you through the hard times and now you may feel as if you have to do this alone. 'Alone' is a terribly lonely word and I think it is a misconception in this case because you are surrounded by love and light at all times. You have your spirit loved ones, ancestors, guardian angel and spirit guides with you even in the loneliest hour. Try not to think of yourself as 'alone' at all. Imagine yourself wrapped in the wings of an angel that embraces and protects you. Relax and feel safe. You might wish to call upon a specific angel such as Archangel Michael, who is especially good at offering protection and reassurance, or you may prefer to feel the loving embrace of your spirit loved one either in the form of arms or wings. I will talk more about this in the chapter on angels.

You may find that one of the most comforting things you can do is learn to meditate and connect with the angels and spirits that lovingly surround you. One good way of doing this involves soaking in a warm bath containing sea salt. Light a candle where you will be able to see it, as you relax in the soothing water. Also burn some incense in the room, where you will be able to gaze lazily at the smoke trail. Breathing deeply let all the tension go from your body and allow yourself to become more and more relaxed. Gazing at the candle you may begin to see patterns or even an angelic figure in the flame. Maybe the delicate trail of incense smoke will also invoke spiritual images in your mind. Try to clear away all thoughts and empty your mind and then listen for angelic or spiritual guidance. You may sense your loved one or an angel speaking to you in your mind. Maybe you will feel them sending you love or giving you advice. Perhaps you will shed tears of joy or relief as you sense them draw near to you. Don't worry if you do not manage to achieve very much the first time you try this but do persist as spirit communication happens so much more readily when you are able to achieve a state of deep relaxation. For this reason many people have their first or most profound spiritual encounters just before they fall asleep or just as they are waking. This kind of twilight state offers spirit an optimum level of communication as you are most attuned to them at these moments.

Doreen Virtue's 'Connecting with your Angels kit' is a good starting point if you would like some help with this exercise.

Part of your self-healing might involve developing your spiritual and mediumistic skills so that you more readily and more confidently hear or sense spirit contact. This route is not for everybody but it is I believe available to everybody and some of you reading this book already know that you have the potential to develop mediumship skills. This is not a suggestion that you have a change of career and decide to become a professional medium. I merely suggest that you might enjoy optimizing your ability to communicate with your loved ones in spirit. If you feel the need for support during this journey of unfolding your powers you might like to join a local Spiritualist Church or join a group of like-minded people sitting in a spiritualist medium circle. There is nothing to fear, love surrounds and protects you at all times.

Spiritual healing can also be a most marvelous experience. I was lucky enough to attend a healing at the Arthur Findlay College in Stanstead England where I received the most beautiful healing session from a very gifted healer. As I entered the room nervously, unsure what would be involved in healing I was asked to fill out a short questionnaire and sit and wait for a healer to become available. As I looked around the room I could see all the recipients were experiencing something quite phenomenal during their healings and I was particularly drawn to one of the healers. It didn't seem that she would be the one to heal me but somehow the order of the queue was shuffled and she stepped forward to greet me and invite me for a healing. A few times in your life you will be fortunate enough to stand in the presence of somebody you know at once is a magically good person. Their aura will captivate you and you can sense they have a power beyond the normal range. The first time that I was in the presence of somebody like this, I felt I knew at last the true meaning of 'charisma', it is something quite amazing and almost indescribable. When I first met a man with this type of aura I felt I knew what it must have felt like to be in the presence of Jesus as he moved among the people. The lady who now stood before me had the aura of an angel and the looks of a Native American Indian healing woman. She looked at my form and glanced at the reason I had asked for a healing, where I had simply written 'bereavement'. She embraced me briefly and asked me to sit down. She told me to relax and close my eyes and that I would know when she was finished as she would touch me gently on the shoulders. What followed can only be described as miraculous and was I believe a true religious experience. I could not see but could sense her healing hands hovering over my body and as she worked I became aware of a large angel standing behind me placing its wings in such a way that it would appear that they came from my own shoulders. I then became aware of my husband's love emanating from in front of me and could sense each of my heavenly spirit babies sitting on my shoulders. Tears streamed hot and fast down my cheeks with relief, joy, love and healing but they did not come with sobs or crying it was just the same beautiful relief that I had seen others experiencing in the room earlier. When the healing was over she touched me gently on the shoulders and gave me some water to drink, bringing me gently back to the moment. When I recovered my composure from this very emotional healing, I stood up and embraced this magical woman as though she were my oldest friend. I really can't thank her enough for her kindness and the generosity she has in sharing her gift of healing with others. You can request a healing at any Spiritualist church.

There are many forms of complementary therapies that you might like to incorporate into your self-healing. Aromatherapy for example has a lot to offer throughout your life's development and specifically during bereavement; you might find a consultation with an experienced recommended Aromatherapist beneficial. If this feels too much for you at the moment financially or emotionally you might like to try the following home remedies:

Get yourself a simple oil burner where you light a candle under a small reservoir of water and drip a few drops of oil into the water to diffuse into your room. Neroli oil is known to be extremely beneficial during bereavement; it comes from a type of orange tree and is known to be both spiritually uplifting and relaxing. A few drops in a burner will fill your environment with beautiful fragrance. Neroli is known as the number one oil for stress and shock and grief. It is also used to treat disorientation, fright, hysteria, mental strain, overwork, and restlessness with exhaustion. All emotions we are likely to encounter in our road to readjustment. Other useful oils include Rose and Frankincense. Rose oil is an expensive but very worthwhile addition to your self-healing resources. You can blend it with Neroli or frankincense or use it alone in a burner or a few drops blended with bath oil in the bath. Rose oil is considered to be the queen of flower oils and is indicated for bereavement where you feel lost in the past, as well as for fear, grief, nerves, regret, sadness, and terror. Frankincense has long been recognized for its spiritual value hence its value as a gift to Jesus at his birth. Frankincense can be used for spiritual protection and is highly recommended for bereavement and 'prolonged' grief as well as courage, fear, insecurity, nerves, nightmares, panic attacks, paranoia, perseverance in difficult circumstances, security, self criticism, and stability. These three oils can be dropped into your bath, vaporized in your room or blended with spring water and a few drops of alcohol to make a room spray. If you wish to make an uplifting room spray collect some rose petals and soak them in hot water until the water becomes filled with color and scent. Strain the petals off and reserve the water, you can add other flowers to the mixture such as jasmine or honeysuckle or any other flower available to you. Add a few drops of alcohol as a preservative and dilute with water. You can then put the mixture into a plant mister and add a few drops of aromatherapy oils to make a beautiful room fragrance. Keep this in the fridge between uses. This spray especially if blended with a few drops of Frankincense is an excellent spray to free your atmosphere of any unwanted spiritual activity or to help you feel relaxed about spirit contact. Frankincense will protect you at all times.

If you can persuade somebody to give you a healing massage, you may also enjoy blending a few drops of each essential oil in carrier oil such as almond oil. Measure your carrier oil carefully to work out the number of drops of neat essential oils to add. For example 20 ml of carrier oil can have half that number of drops of essential oil added to it; therefore it can have up to 10 drops of oil. 10mls of carrier oil would have 5 drops of essential oil added; 50ml of carrier oil could have 25 drops added and so on. Be careful when blending oils as some smell much stronger than others and will therefore be needed in smaller quantities. Do not exceed the half drops to ml ratio rule or you might experience skin irritation.

Always be sure to buy reputable oils of a good quality and sold in dark glass bottles, which are to be kept away from the light. Never use undiluted aromatherapy oils directly on your skin. (The exceptions to this rule being lavender and tea tree oils, which can be used, undiluted in small quantities for first aid use if necessary). Pregnant women and those suffering from epilepsy should take professional advice before using aromatherapy oils. I will recommend further reading at the end of the book for those wishing to explore Aromatherapy further.

Another therapy that might help with your healing is Crystal Healing. Crystals are filled with natures healing energy and power and simply having them in your environment can be both uplifting and calming. You can either visit a qualified Crystal Healing Therapist or work with crystals at home. Here are some basic ideas, which might help and you can find much more information in Judy Hall's excellent guide to crystals: *'The Crystal Bible'*. You may even find that you become sufficiently intrigued by the wonderful power of crystals that you decide to pursue a course in crystal healing and become a healer yourself.

Amethyst is a crystal, which most people can readily identify by its beautiful purple color and it is readily available and comparatively inexpensive. As well as promoting spiritual awareness, Amethyst is a very balancing stone and can help you to get back on an even keel. You can use it to help you release anger, fear and anxiety and come to terms with sadness, grief and loss. Amethyst can relieve pain on every level, spiritual, physical, emotional and psychological and you can benefit from it either in jewellery or as geodes or stones in your environment. Amethysts tend to fade in sunlight. You can place one under your pillow if you are suffering from insomnia or nightmares.

Azurite is another useful stone for self-healing and can help clear stress, worry, grief and sadness. You can also use it to guide your psychic and intuitive development. Judy Hall notes that:

> "It urges the soul towards enlightenment. It cleanses and stimulates the third eye and attunes to spiritual guidance. This crystal allows journeys out of the body to take place easily and safely. It raises consciousness to a higher level and gives greater control over spiritual unfoldment. It facilitates a meditative and channeling state."

Hence you might find multiple benefits from investing in some Azurite, as you may be able to use it during meditation to raise your awareness of your spirit loved ones and help with the communication process.

Judy also recommends Sugilite, of which she says:

> "This loving stone protects the soul from shocks, trauma and disappointments and relieves spiritual tension...Sugilite can help bring light and love into the darkest situations.... Sugilite imparts the ability to face up to unpleasant matters. It alleviates sorrow, grief and fear and promotes self-forgiveness...place on the third eye to alleviate despair."

The third eye is the chakra center found between your two physical eyes and is thought to be the source of inner vision and intuition. As you study crystal healing you will automatically get drawn into chakra balancing, clearing and healing as the two are entwined. Chakra balancing can be a very helpful aid to your self-healing and I highly recommend Doreen virtue's meditation CD '*Chakra clearing*'.

Chapter six

RECOGNIZING OUR OWN IMMORTALITY

When I set out to write this book, it was to share with the world, the comfort of knowing that our loved ones continue in spirit, and that our separation from them is an illusion. One of the most healing things that can happen to a grieving person is the sure and certain knowledge that their loved one *lives on* spiritually and that their personality survives after death. This is where a good spiritualist medium can be so helpful, allowing our departed loved ones to provide real evidence, of survival of the personality after physical death. Even if you have been blessed with many contacts from your loved one on a day to day basis, it can still be an amazing experience to hear from them through a skilled medium. It confirms what you already believe to be true; that we do not die.

This single belief has made the continuation of *my* life, after the death of my husband possible. Without that faith I do not know how I would have picked up the pieces of my life and carried on. Faith can conquer seemingly insurmountable obstacles; it moves mountains and saves lives. I am not talking about any particular religion or faith but the possession of a 'knowingness' that we are not alone and that God, spirit, a universal source energy or a communal force greater than ourselves, exists and that life has meaning. Whether your faith is based on a particular religion, or on ideas and intuitions that you have conceived yourself, in the light of inner reflection and experience, the result can be the same. Faith can quite simply bring comfort in our darkest hours and a reason and the courage to carry on. The most comforting of faiths support us by bringing us the belief and understanding that we are more than flesh and blood, much more in fact. I believe that a personal belief system of some sort is fundamental to our recovery from life's challenges and losses. Without a belief in the continuance of spirit after physical death, I feel that both grieving and adjustment must be much more difficult to deal with. A whole rich source of joy and reassurance would be missing from the recovery process.

I believe that our belief system is not something fixed and inflexible, not something that we can learn once and feel that we know it all. I feel sure that it is our life's journey to evolve our beliefs a little more each day. Like a scientist trying and testing a thousand theories before discovering what seems to them, to be the indisputable truth; we can evaluate our experiences through life, searching for the 'truth' and meaning of it all.

We can connect to our higher selves, our higher knowing, our angels and spirit to make incredible leaps in this knowledge and belief system. Such leaps of the 'Eureka!' type may not come very frequently, but when they do they can rock your world. If you are fortunate enough to have one of those revelations, that maybe will help all humanity, let it also pass that you find the means and the will and the motivation to share your great insight and God-given revelation with the world.

Writing this book should have been far easier for me than it was in reality. In theory I knew why I was writing the book: to help others and to share the healing knowledge that had helped me so much, yet something continually held me back from finishing the book for nearly a year. It was as if the first chapters were almost dictated by angels, yet a chapter seemed to elude me. A year later I found out why.

The missing part of the puzzle was how we can deal with our own physical mortality.

I have written and learned much about how to deal with the loss of our loved ones, by tuning into their presence at our sides in spirit, and how to recognize, accept and love their communication. However, although I had touched upon the comfort to be had between loved ones, during a seemingly terminal illness, if they believed in life after death; I hadn't truly been able to feel that knowledge from the perspective of the dying person.

Okay so this was the missing part of my advice to you, the missing section of the book and trust the universe to deliver me the answer.

A short time ago, I began to constantly see my father in unusual locations such as at a traffic light or passing by on a bicycle. The strange thing about this was that the sightings were more like spirit sightings, than those of seeing a physical being and what was more, my father was thousands of miles away in another country entirely. These sightings naturally began to worry me and play on my mind. Was my father in some danger? I couldn't get it from my mind that I absolutely had to see my father. Money was extremely scarce and so I asked my angels to help make a journey to see him possible. True to form the angels soon made sure that I found free flights for myself, and two of my children, to fly home to England to be with my parents for a week.

I almost dreaded what state I would find him in, as my desire to see him was so strong and felt like an un-ignorable warning. So imagine my surprise when I arrived in England to find him looking absolutely great. What a relief I felt but I couldn't help but wonder why I had been so strongly guided to journey to see him. The answer to this came when he ironically recognized an illness in me, and insisted that I go to the doctors as soon as I returned to Spain. If it hadn't been for his insight and advice I wouldn't have bothered my doctor with what seemed like fairly trivial symptoms and wouldn't have known until far too late, that I had all the signs of colon cancer. Tumor markers in my blood initiated a series of urgent investigations and I found myself having to cope now with the almost certain probability that I had cancer.

There was me thinking my huge link to spirit and my mediumship, were a gift given to help my husband stay in contact and to know that he would never have to leave us, as well as a gift to help me to bring loved ones through to others. I had never seriously given time to the thought that it might also be to help me come to terms with my own physical mortality.

Okay so what emotions does a person pass through when they learn they have or may have cancer or another terminal condition? Shock was pretty high up on my list, swiftly followed by disbelief, denial, anger, helplessness, determination and so on. Of course for a parent ones first thoughts are naturally: what will become of my children? I remember my husband telling his oncologist quite plainly that he simply could not die as he had young children to support. Unfortunately it doesn't work like that.

So how should I try to cope with this huge piece of information? I didn't feel it appropriate to confide in the children just yet, as they had lost one parent to cancer already, and the rest of my family were thousands of miles away. Thank goodness for telephones and emails that can help us feel that our friends and family are with us no matter how far apart we may be. Of course nothing could substitute for having loving arms physically about me at that moment but long distance sympathy and advice was an enormous comfort, as was the knowledge that my loved ones spirit side were also there to support me.

Asking out to my angels I felt guided to take meditative baths and listen to inspirational CDs. This helped to relax my mind and let my higher-self gain control over my natural panic reactions and disquiet. Incense, candles, warm water and soft music all helped to elevate my consciousness and mood to more spiritual plains. It was during one of these deep meditative states that I was given my 'Eureka!' moment; my revelation, my salvation and my inspiration to write this section of the book.

Like a flash of light or insight, I was lifted from my fear and despair and shown the wider picture, the greater truth and I felt as though the room was lit up by angels, pure love and deep peace.

As I was given this revelation I was also given that I should share it with all humankind. It was a message both for me and for every reader of this book and as many people as would listen to it. In essence the revelation was that we cannot die it is impossible.

Lying there in the warm water wondering how my children would manage without me if I died, and how I would cope with the end of my life, this huge revelation was life changing. In that moment I realized that whatever happened to my physical body, I myself would live forever. A profound peace, joy and relief swept through me as I realized, accepted and knew for certain that we cannot die.

We live forever like a light that burns long after the candle has faded and died. We cannot and will not die…that is the joke. My body is mortal but *I am not* and neither my friend are you. There is nothing to worry about, it is like a butterfly struggling free from a chrysalis, our spirit will rise up and away from our physical body which, is no more than a shell that will inevitably have to be discarded one day.

It was plain as day to me when my husband died that the

body that lay before me had nothing to do with him as a person. He was gone from that body but lived on in spirit.

It may help to hold on to this revelation at all times.

This message was transmitted to me directly from what I believe to be angels:

"Every day we are not nearer to death but nearer to being released from our mortal physical body, nearer to the next part of our spiritual journey, nearer to more enlightenment than we can presently imagine. Every day we are nearer to being released into immortality where we will experience a self-relief from the limitations of being confined in our physical body. We should feel able to care for our physical bodies in a loving respectful way, in order to enjoy more time on this plane and in this dimension with our loved ones that are currently in the physical form. But we should know that all apparent separations are temporary. We are one spirit, one love, one energy and we will always be together, we cannot die it is impossible."

Remember that my husband has said through two different mediums that he has learned in a short time in spirit, more than we will ever know in this life. I believe him of course, as making sense of everything here can often seem so hard!

So what can we do to achieve the level of enlightenment where we will feel peace and receive our own moments of revelation?

Meditating cannot be recommended highly enough as a means to enlightenment as are a healthy diet and lifestyle.

Val Williams comments in her book `Two worlds as one', published by Red Wing publishing:

"You and I are still children you know, for each day of our lives there is something to learn, hurdles to overcome, new truths to establish, and many times we reach out to other people to help us, to give us some understanding and we find ourselves disappointed. WHY do that, when there is a source of knowledge that is close to you that can help you better than any other living person possibly can? Establish for yourself your link with your own soul, through quiet times, through meditation perhaps, and learn that the voices within you and the thoughts that won't go away are the guidance you need."

Let us learn to see only the light in one another, because only this Divine light and love really exist. Everything else is temporary and therefore an illusion, only spirit and love which are one with God and unite every living being, has any meaning at all.

It may be hard to detach ourselves from the physical and material aspects of life and the world in which we live, but learning to see light and love in each person and see past their physical form, can bring great joy and enlightenment. It also brings us the certain knowledge that we can never be parted from those we love, we will exist in spirit together for all time. Many believe that we may even reincarnate with the same loved ones in many lifetimes. This would make sense of past life regressions in which we find ourselves in different roles but incarnated with some of the same souls. We can recognize each other as the eyes stay the same through time; the light and the essence of each soul remain recognizable.

Remember how I met and recognized my late husband during my psychic journey in chapter three.

Know that we live forever and great comfort will be yours.

CHAPTER 7

ANGELS

The subject of angels could fill many books on its own, but for now I will try and express the strength and support that they can afford you during your bereavement and other difficult periods of your life. For me, angels have been a lifesaver; God's beautiful messengers work tirelessly to support everyone that asks for their help. Therein lays the key: you do have to ask! Free will means that the angels will never interfere in your life, unless you give them permission to help you, with the exception of life threatening situations before your time. Once you call them to your side and ask for their assistance they will do everything in their power to bring about what you need. This could be your emotional, spiritual and physical healing, or a specific request such as new sources of support in your life, new friends, a new job or a new home; whatever you need. Maybe you will ask that your faith in the eternal nature of love and life be strengthened, or that your belief in the afterlife could be validated in some way. You could ask for evidence that your loved one lives on in spirit or you might simply ask for strength.

Have no fear that you offend God in some way by praying to his angels or calling them to you; they are his Divine messengers and just like all of us they are one with God. They will never bring you anything that is not for your highest good and they may bring your wishes to fruition in unexpected and creative ways. Angels are part of the synchronicity we so often see at work, those amazing 'coincidences' that bring so much good into our lives.

An example of angels at work was very evident to me when Jo came into my life. We first met when she came to see me for a parent teacher interview, concerned about her son Tom. I was his new teacher and she wanted me to know a little background information regarding her charming son who at the age of ten, despite great intelligence had yet to have any success or happiness in school. He had found his early years in a Spanish-speaking classroom a nightmare and had made little progress. He was now enrolled in the international British speaking school in which I would be his teacher but, until now had still been very unhappy. I had been teaching Tom for about a week and had already been amazed by his psychic ability. When I had taken on this classroom on the retirement of the previous teacher mid-year, I had been appalled by the sadness and drab décor in which I was expected to work and so I set about making it a more beautiful and inspiring environment for me and my students. There was a large notice board behind my desk and I had the urge to place an angel poster there but could not think of any educational excuse to do so. The first time Tom approached my desk he looked in to my eyes and said:

"Miss Deborah, you should have an angel poster on that notice board."

This was an amazing experience for me, and Tom and I were connected in a special sense from that moment on. He always seemed to be able to read my thoughts and feelings and knew just what to say. He seemed far wiser than his ten years.

When I met his mother, Jo, for the first time at the parent-teacher meeting, I felt I had to tell her about Tom's special gift. She was delighted but not surprised and said that she was a great believer in angels and had asked them to bring a very special teacher in to Tom's life, and that she believed that was why I had joined the school. I was stunned because she was the first person I had met who was also working with angels in her life and we became instant friends.

During our time together Tom transformed from a student who was convinced he didn't understand and couldn't do anything, to one of the highest achievers in the class, in just six months.

"You switched on a light in Tom", commented his mother, and Tom continues to go from strength to strength. He is an exceptionally talented young man now and amazes all who come in to contact with him. I of course was honored to be a catalyst for Tom and many other students who made great leaps that year and I thank the angels for the synchronicity that had bought us all together. I had called on them urgently for a job and found myself employed at the school the very next day! Jo had called for someone to help her son and everything just gelled together.

Tom and his family were suffering the bereavement of Tom's brother Josh and I had recently lost my husband. We all united to give each other emotional support and this transpired to be a key relationship in my healing process. Jo regularly spent hours on the telephone, helping me with the grieving process and talking me down from suicide. I will never be able to thank her enough. My gift to her was helping Tom achieve his potential and also on occasions I was privileged to be able to bring messages through from Josh. I credit our finding each other at the right time to our angels.

On what would have been Josh's eighteenth birthday he actually managed to affect me so strongly that I was thrown to the floor and writhed in agony for some time as he showed me how he had suffered. I was left unable to move and my frightened children had to lift me on to the sofa and wait for me to come round. During this frightening visit I should have asked spirit to take the pain away from me but it all happened so intensely that I was lost in the experience. I asked Josh what his message was and what I needed to know. He told me to tell Jo she was his number one mum and then a sense of peace came over me and he was gone.

When I recovered from this unsettling visit, I contacted Jo and conveyed the message just as Josh had instructed me to. She was overwhelmed.

"I was his step mum really but he always told me I was 'his number one mum'". We both cried. There are few things as moving or reassuring to hear from spirit than well known phrases, private jokes, special songs and so on as the provide real evidence that we live on.

All this happened I believe because both Jo and I were calling to angels for help and our two sets of needs collided to bring much joy all round. Thank you, angels.

Okay, so how can angels help during bereavement? I believe that if you call upon them with sincerity either through thought, prayer, speaking aloud or writing, your request will be heard and answered. You might want to ask for something specific such as a greater awareness of spirit around you, emotional strength, guidance or support, or you may simply call out

"Angels please help me!"

Angels go to work immediately on our behalf and rest assured they always work within the will of God and for our highest good. If you are feeling lonely or afraid you can call extra angels to your side in an instant. If I am facing a difficult situation such as a surgical procedure or a difficult interview, I often ask for a thousand angels to surround and support me. You can do this when grief becomes overwhelming too, or simply ask for daily support from angels and feel their wings wrap about you.

There is no request too big or too trivial for the angels, they will happily assist with anything you desire whether it is a safe journey, a parking space or a new soul mate. There is nothing that you cannot achieve with their help if it is for your highest good. Feel safe. We are never alone, angels and God and our spirit guides and spirit loved ones go with us wherever we may go.

In 1990 my late husband Peter was driving home from visiting his first wife, as she lay very sick in a hospice. Perhaps due to his mind being elsewhere or through a twist of fate, he became involved in a terrible traffic accident. Pulling out to overtake a foreign Lorry, he found himself sandwiched between two enormous juggernauts which flipped his car over and over and over until the car was thrown clear of the road and landed upside down, without a single piece of glass left intact. Trapped in the car, which had been squashed to a fraction of its normal size, all logic said that he should be dead. At that moment Peter recalls an angelic presence or the voice of God telling him that he could not pass to spirit yet because he had 'more work to do'. Within an instant a nurse and a fireman arrived at the scene. Remarkably they had been traveling in the two cars behind Peter and had seen everything. Peter had multiple head injuries and was peppered with shards of glass but he made a perfect recovery. He often recounted this story to me during our years together and he always said the same thing:

"I was mystified when God said I had more work to do, until I met you and I knew I was meant to look after you and the children. It wasn't my time."

I also credit the angels with having saved my second son Kingsley's life when he was a newborn baby. Angels and angels in human form or earth angels often seem to have a miraculous way of appearing at crucial moments and then simply disappearing. When Kingsley was born after a very difficult delivery he was put into my arms like dead meat. I was panic stricken at the sight of this listless baby who to me seemed to need reviving and special attention. My first child had been born writhing, crying, gurgling and looking for food. Kingsley quite honestly looked near deathly. I screamed at the midwives to revive him or check him over or get him moving but they simply laughed and said

"You had post natal depression with your first son didn't you?"

As though this meant I was some hysterical woman over-reacting. In the days that followed Kingsley did not improve and I just knew something was wrong. Every time a member of staff appeared I asked them to look at Kingsley because he was not well and without exception they all ignored my plight and put it down to post-natal depression. This was terrifying. I hadn't been depressed with Daniel until he was six months old and I was an intelligent second time mother, who knew the difference between a healthy baby and one that was in serious need of attention. I handled Kingsley as infrequently as possible as I didn't want to get attached to him; I really felt he was going to die. The terror of this not being taken seriously defies description but I really felt helpless to convince anyone that he was not well.

A few days later Kingsley and I were waiting in a hospital corridor to be shown how to give a baby a bath. As we were waiting, a Doctor I had never seen before walked past Kingsley as he lay in his transparent plastic cot. Suddenly she was screaming and it seemed like all hell was being let loose. She was shouting at the entire staff:

"Why isn't this baby in Special Care?"

Within minutes Kingsley was being rushed round to the special care baby unit where his life would be saved.

The Doctor seemed to disappear as miraculously as she had arrived and despite another nine days in the hospital I never saw her again. No one seemed to know who she was, and I was never able to thank her. To this day I believe she was an angel in human form.

When my husband was very ill, my daughter Elizabeth and I prayed for angels to help him and in particular we prayed to Archangel Raphael to send healing as he is heaven's highest healing angel. A few days later Elizabeth was lucky enough to see two angels flying past and she later identified them from paintings as Archangels Sandalphon and Metatron. This made sense as both these archangels would have been very pertinent to her at such a young age. I will explain more about specific angels and their specialties in a moment. When the angels flashed past Elizabeth and I, I perceived them only as angelic lights but she was lucky enough to see them in real detail.

The only time I was privileged to see angels in such detail was in a very religious experience I had which occurred the last time my husband and Peter and I made love. He was so ill that I had long given up on the idea that we might be able to express our love physically one more time, but we were truly blessed with a very special night about a week before he died. I can honestly say that I not only saw but also heard heavenly angels and the whole room lit up. It was the nearest I have ever been to God and I thank the angels so much for that very special experience. Love truly is the highest power in the universe. The joy we beheld in that moment was like a gift from God.

You can call upon angels to sustain, help and guide you at any time. You might at the same time like to ask your own guardian angel and your spirit loved ones to support you too.

I also thank and credit the angels for bringing other special friends into my life when I have most needed them. Unfortunately when we suffer bereavement some of our friends tend to disappear from our lives. This is one of those crucial times in life when we really find out who our friends are, and it can be surprising to find that those you least expected would desert you in your hour of need are nowhere to be seen. Often if you have been part of a couple or a social group for a long time the dynamics of your social life can change so much that you find yourself dropped from dinner parties and other social functions. I have heard many people comment that a widow or widower are quickly seen as a `threat ′in social situations, as though we have become sex-starved marriage-breakers over night! This is as hurtful as it is ridiculous, and you may feel very rightfully aggrieved to be treated in this way. Similarly if you have lost a child, you may find that other parents of terminally ill children, who once seemed such great friends to you whilst you were facing similar challenges, may shy away from you now. This is hurtful but the other parents are protecting themselves from your grief, they simply cannot handle it.

Fortunately there are many more people out there in support groups and in your local community who do have an idea what you are going through because they have been down a similar road. This source of new friends may offer you more strength than your old friends are capable of offering right now. Trust God and the angels to guide you to these sources of support, and know that one day you will feel strong enough to offer support to others in return.

You might like to light a white candle and relax through deep breathing and then ask out to the angels

"Angels please send true friends and earth angels to my side to help me now. Please help me to recognize these wonderful people and to fully accept all the help that they offer. It is a blessing to receive and a blessing to allow others to give. I accept loving support and guidance now."

Do not feel that you burden others or that you are a nuisance. People love to help, they love to give and they receive joy and love in return. You will be amazed at who the angels will lovingly guide in to your life.

I believe that angels guided my wonderful friends Raphael and Tania into my life at the perfect moment. We had lived in the same Spanish town for years without ever becoming acquainted when a mutual friend Helen, introduced us all. An instant friendship was forged and as we got to know one another I was diagnosed with colon cancer. Already widowed and caring for 4 school-aged children this was a shocking blow to me as you can imagine. Worse still, was that after successful colon surgery I was informed it had now metastasized to my liver. The initial panic had me imagining all sorts of worst-case scenarios and Tania and Raphael were quick to rush to my aid, talking to me and visiting me every day and turning up to clean my house and keep me sane. Can you believe that these two special new friends were both trained nurses and that Raphael had been a chemotherapy nurse? The only friends I have ever had that were nurses were guided in to my life just before a cancer diagnosis. I would like to thank the angels for being so wise, and thank Tania and Raphael for being two of my earth angels.

Never be afraid to ask the angels to guide loving friends to your side, and learn to keep your heart open to receive love, comfort and happiness no matter how much you are hurting at this moment.

When Doreen, a counselor whose story is told in the chapter `Making it count', visited a client for the first time who had recently lost his son, she was greeted with a lot of anger and animosity.

"I don't know why you are here, you can't possibly know what it feels like to lose a son!" he shouted angrily.

Doreen could see that he was in terrible emotional pain and was not put off by his surly manner and aggressive tone.

"I do not know how you feel after losing your son, but I do know how I felt when I lost my daughter." She replied quietly. The huge man burst into tears and they embraced. He realized she had been sent to him for a very special reason and that she really would be able to help. I like to think that the angels brought them together that day, perhaps encouraged by their two

children in spirit. Nobody knows for sure, but I am convinced that miracles happen like this every day when spirit and angels get to work through the loving hearts of those on earth. Never be afraid to ask for help or to reach out to another heart. I do believe that it is true that we should treat others as we would wish to be treated, and that we do reap what we sow; giving and receiving help is all one, it is all part of the mighty power of our oneness with each other, it is all part of love.

Many religions including Christianity, Judaism and Islam include angels or angelic beings in their philosophy, and whilst we may argue about many aspects of religion, everybody loves angels; in monotheistic religion they are the Divine messengers of God. However much religions agree or disagree, angels are non-denominational and help people of all beliefs and backgrounds. Just as there is one God no matter by what name he is known, there are universal angelic messengers who mediate between us and the Divine.

Doreen Virtue explains in detail in her book 'Angels 101' published by Hay House Inc in 2006, all about angels and their history. She also points out that in surveys in the United States up to 85% of adults reported believing in angels and 32% said that they had experienced angelic encounters. She concludes therefore that it is perfectly normal to believe in angels! Doreen works as an angel therapist and trains others to do the same; she has seen remarkable improvements in her clients' lives when they call upon angels:

> "Those who regularly contact their angels…feel happier, more peaceful and confident, and less afraid of death or the future. They know that they are not alone, because they have trust-worthy guardians watching over them…Those who work with angels develop a closer relationship with God, as (they) heal fears and guilt that they may have absorbed from religious teachings."

Doreen Virtue goes on to explain in detail just about everything you could wish to know about angels, their hierarchies and which specific archangels you may wish to call upon according to your needs. I would recommend that if you wish to explore angels in greater depth you obtain some of her angel books and resources published by Hay House, that I will recommend at the end of the book.

If you wish to call upon an angel or archangel that has special powers in a particular field here is a guide, but you may call upon many or any angels at any time so do not feel limited by this list.

If you are feeling insecure, afraid or in need of strength and protection it is a good idea to call Archangel Michael to your side, in an instant he will make sure that you are safe from harm and fill you with reassurance. Michael is often considered the most powerful of all the archangels and appears in the religious texts of Christianity, Judaism and Islam performing heroic acts of protection. I call upon him daily to help me with feeling strong, safe and protected and he has often let me know that he is around in times of need. For example several times when I have been stuck in traffic or anxious during a journey or in danger of collision I have miraculously found myself following a vehicle that has Archangel Michael in some form or other in its advertising. Most frequently this occurs when a delivery lorry finds its way in to my path with San Miguel emblazoned all over it, which of course is Spanish for Saint Michael or Archangel Michael as I call him. On another occasion I was in Madrid with my partner Alexander, when we found ourselves in La Plaza del Sol, which I had visited many times in search of the famous Spanish statue of a bear and a tree. For some reason, probably the volume of tourists milling around, or pressure of time I had never seen the statue, (if you have visited Madrid you might find this incredible as it is in fact in plain sight). However on this occasion I was overwhelmed and delighted to finally see the statue and

Alexander posed for a photograph, reaching up to place his hand on the platform where the bear stood. As he did so he felt a piece of card beneath his fingers and he picked it up to look at it. We were both delighted and amazed to find it was a picture of Archangel Michael as we had felt him with us on many occasions, and often called upon him to help us with our relationship and other issues. Tears pricked at our eyes as we marveled at how unlikely it was that we should find that picture in such busy place where so many stopped to be photographed. Stranger still was that I had always wanted to see the bear and until that moment had never managed to do so. That card of our special San Miguel as we call him here in Spain, has remained with us ever since and now adorns the family car for extra protection!

On other occasions I perceive him as a purple light and know that he is with me. Each Archangel is associated with various colors and crystals that you can use to help summon them when you feel the need of some extra help. Michael may also bring extra angels known as his Band of Mercy if you ask him. I use amethyst when I wish to communicate with Michael through meditation but you really do not need to add anything to yourself to speak to angels. Simply visualize them and communicate through thought and prayer, or ask out aloud for their help or write them a letter. Angels do not mind how we communicate with them and they are always eager to help. Like God they can be with an infinite number of people simultaneously, so you are never depriving someone else of their support.

For healing Archangel Raphael is the supreme healer and is associated with an emerald green healing light. Green candles and green crystals can enhance your feeling of closeness with this special archangel, or simply visualize emerald green and ask him to bathe you in his healing light. You can ask him to heal you or another and he works well with Archangel Michael to help cleanse you of physical or emotional pain. Raphael also helps healers in their work and so you can call upon him to help you if healing others is part of your journey or life purpose. For now simply ask him to soothe you with an emerald green healing balm and release you from the pain of grief. Again Doreen Virtue has some incredible guided meditations that can help you with this for example the audio CD Angel Therapy Meditations, Hay House audio 2008. Raphael along with Michael and Gabriel is one of the three sainted angels and therefore you may also see him referred to as Saint Raphael or San Raphael.

A particularly helpful archangel to call upon during times of bereavement is Archangel Azrael because he helps escort departed souls to heaven and heals the grief stricken. He also supports those who work with or console the bereaved and is sometimes referred to as the "angel of death". You may like to call Azrael to your side when grieving becomes especially difficult, or simply ask that he be with you throughout your healing journey. Also when you are thinking of your loved one in spirit you can ask for extra healing for them as they progress spirit side.

If you are having difficulty expressing your emotions regarding your loss, call Archangel Gabriel to your side and wear moonstone crystals at your throat chakra. Gabriel is God's messenger angel and can help you with all forms of communication, whether it be expressing yourself verbally to others, or writing down your experiences. You can also ask her to help bring messages between you and your spirit loved one and open your channels of communication.

Archangel Haniel may also help you with communication with spirit, as she is known to enhance clairvoyance. She can also help women when hormonal shifts and cycles add to life's challenges. When you feel weepy and off-balance call upon Haniel to aid your healing.

Archangel Jeremiel can further aid your emotional healing, and help you to take stock of your new life and make any necessary adjustments. Call upon him to help you forgive the past and make positive plans for the future. At first your grief may have you praying simply for the strength to live one day or one minute at a time, but eventually you will be ready to make a review of your life without the physical presence of your loved one, and be ready to consider making some changes.

If your new life poses financial difficulties, because of the loss of income associated with your loved one during their physical lifetime, you may wish to call upon Archangel Ariel. Ariel helps provide for our physical needs such as food, shelter and money and so if this has become an issue for you for any reason, do not hesitate to call her to your side. I know that when my husband died I was for a time left with four children to raise and no income and yet the angels and I believe Peter himself, were quick to resolve my problems by providing me with almost immediate employment. Remember that our spirit loved ones work like angels to guide and assist us and are never far away. Call them, speak to them or think of them and they will let you know that they are right beside you working to help with your day to day life for as long as you need them.

If you find as I did, that bereavement has made it difficult to keep your house or your possessions in order, or you feel chaos creeping in to any area of your life, call upon Archangel Jophiel. Jophiel helps beautify your environment and bring order, peace and harmony to your home. If housework has become a seemingly insurmountable challenge during your healing, ask her to help bring new order and tranquility. Having become almost housework-phobic after my husband passed to spirit, I eventually over came the problem by no longer calling it 'cleaning 'or 'tidying' or 'housework' or 'chores', but instead began to think of it as 'beautifying' my home, and I asked Jophiel to help me. Psychologically I find it easier to say that I am going to beautify my kitchen or bathroom, than to tell myself I must wash the dishes and clean the toilet! Simple changes of attitude can make all the difference to our happiness and the angels are always ready to help.

If you have lost a child or you are trying to help grief-stricken children, call upon Archangel Metatron. Metatron works closely with children, especially those with extra needs such as learning difficulties or special gifts, or those facing bereavement and other challenges. He also takes special care of our children in heaven and helps support parents. Call upon him for any strength and support you need regarding your children at this difficult time. I know that for us as a family in the months following the death of my husband, relationships and family harmony were very difficult.

Archangel Raguel can be called upon to bring harmony to relationships and may be a very useful friend to you all during the difficult adjustment to new family dynamics. Whether it be rebellious grieving teenagers or feuding relatives you can always call upon the angels to help restore peace and harmony. Remember that each of you is grieving in your own way and that the natural anger that follows bereavement means that relationships are often especially volatile at this time. Ask Raguel and he will happily work on this for the highest good and happiness of all involved.

If you are finding spirit communication difficult, call Archangel Raziel to your side. Raziel can help you to heal any psychic or spiritual blocks that are preventing you from enjoying all the contact that your spirit loved one may be attempting to make. Ask Raziel to open your senses to spirit messages and to help you enjoy and interpret any dream visits you may be blessed with, in which your loved one literally visits you as you sleep. I have been lucky enough to have many dream visits which are quite unlike ordinary dreams because they are so vivid. You can request a dream visit at anytime simply by praying or asking out as you settle down to sleep. Your loved one will be delighted to spend time with you as you sleep.

If on the other hand you are finding spirit communication

unsettling, frightening or unwelcome, call upon Archangel Zadkiel. Zadkiel works with Archangel Michael to help release us from lower energies; so if you feel that spirit contact is of a negative kind, or you simply don't feel comfortable with it at present, call upon these two protective angels immediately.

Archangel Uriel will help you open up to the idea of spirit communication when you are ready. He is the angel of light and will help illuminate your mind to infinite possibilities and new ideas, if you ask him to. Everything will unfold for your highest good in perfect timing. Trust God, the universe and the angels to enlighten and heal and protect you perfectly.

You are never alone, your spirit loved ones, guardian angel, spirit guides, God and the angels walk beside you always.

Your own personal guardian angel is appointed to you at birth and will guide and protect you until you return home to spirit. If you wish to meet your spirit guide there are many excellent ways to do this including self-hypnotic psychic journeys and guided meditations. I especially recommend Tony Stockwell's Audio CD guided meditation 'Meditation to help you meet your spirit guide', available from New World Music.

For connecting with your angels I recommend Doreen Virtue's books, cards and audio CDs available from Hay House.

For being in contact with your spirit loved ones I simply recommend opening your heart to them and allowing them to be with you.

Chapter 8

PROTECTION FROM SPIRIT AND GUARDIAN ANGELS

Hopefully, through your own experiences and by reading this book, you have learned to feel comfortable with communication from spirit. If not, relax; a sense of safety will come to you.

Sometimes it is difficult to know whether feelings and intuitions we get come from our spirit loved ones, our own inner guidance or from guardian angels, either way the result is always positive and sometimes life saving.

I would like to share with you some examples in which lives were saved or altered through some kind of Divine intervention. Whether this be from spirits or angels is impossible to say. See what you think.

Alexander Proenza grew up in Cuba; one day during his childhood, he was walking backwards in a field when he suddenly felt forced to stop and stand very still. He has never forgotten this moment; because when he turned around he realized that he was teetering on the edge of a very deep well, in which he would surely have drowned had he taken one more step. Alexander puts this down to having spirit or angels with him that day, and has also been saved from near death on many other occasions including once when he was viciously attacked by a man with a knife, he escaped miraculously with only arm injuries, even though the attacker was clearly intending a fight to the death.

The Proenza family seems to have wonderful guardian angels about them, as his sister Betty also escaped death. She was the only survivor of a horrific traffic accident.

When my husband was alive, he loved to drive and he was very good at it. Always confident and sure of himself and very skilled he always enjoyed our outings. However, there was one crossroads in the Spanish countryside that always gave him a funny feeling and he mentioned it every time we crossed at that point. He seemed to have a premonition that something would happen there and would cross with extreme caution. During his lifetime we never saw an accident there, but around a year after my husband's death I got a phone call saying that my son Kingsley had been involved in a traffic accident. You can imagine my reaction as my heart sank to hear that he had been taken to hospital. Luckily the car full of teenagers had all had a miraculous escape and when I heard the story I was reminded of Peter's premonition, because it had occurred at that exact crossroads. I listened open-mouthed, as Kingsley related what had happened.

"Mum we weren't drinking or anything and my friend is a really safe driver but we were just coming up to the crossroads when an animal shot out in front of the car and he swerved to miss it. He lost control of the car and we were headed straight at an abandoned house at top speed, I can't explain how, but the doors flew open and David and I were flung from the car before it hit the wall. Those doors have never flown open before and if that hadn't happened I think we would have been killed."

I went cold remembering Peter's foreboding about that cross-roads and felt sure that he had been there to save them that night.

Cars and travel seem particularly involved in spirit or angelic protection, as the next story shows.

I was driving one day with the whole family and we decided to take the toll road, which we rarely did as it was quite expensive. However, we were running a little late and the toll road would save us around an hour's journey. As we headed towards the tollbooths I had a funny feeling that we should wait a few minutes and I said so to the children, who are quite used to me saying such things. As I said this, the car in front of us in the queue, made a u-turn and changed his mind heading for the other road.

"Look that driver just had the same feeling!" I exclaimed.

By this time the children were rather worried and didn't seem to mind when I insisted on waiting a few moments, before going through the toll booth. The same spirit or angel that delayed us then urged me on and we set off down the road. A few minutes later we realized why we had been `told' to wait; there was a horrific accident in which we might well have been involved, had we been on the road a few minutes earlier. I prayed that everyone involved would be cared for by God and we thanked our angels and spirits, as we carried safely on with our journey.

This illustrates how spirit sometimes saves us from disaster in the most unusual ways. For example you may be very annoyed to get a flat tire and miss your plane, until you hear that the plane went down without survivors. Then you will reassess that annoying delay and call it a miracle as it saved your life. God, spirits and angels truly do move in mysterious ways to keep us safe. Your loved one is still protecting you. I have faith that everything happens for a reason.

Messages arrive for us in all sorts of ingenious ways too. A woman who was distraught from traveling between the UK and

New Zealand because her father was seriously ill, prayed to know when he would pass, so that she could be with him at the right time. Spirit urged her to buy a car in New Zealand, to make caring for him easier when she was there. Following this advice she found that her new car had the registration plate END 11 08. From this she knew that heaven was telling her that her father would pass in November 2008, and he did.

Sometimes contact is made through animals or spirit animals, such as the New Zealand man who told his family that when he died he was going with the owl. The family was a bit puzzled because an owl is very rarely seen in New Zealand. However, sure enough a beautiful barn owl appeared at their home one evening, and at that moment the man passed to spirit.

A family dog is likely to be protecting the family long after the animal's passing to spirit and may well help us with our own passing. My cousin Angela received many spirit visits inviting her to pass over when she was very ill, but all were from relatives that she could not remember and so she refused to go. She would recount these experiences like dreams, and one day she confided in her aunty that she had nearly died the previous night and that it was a long, long way to heaven, but when she got there she couldn't stay because her mother wasn't ready to let her go, and so she had to come all the way back. A few evenings later the family dog, from spirit side, came to visit Angela and she recounted this to the family too saying she felt happy about going to heaven now and in a few days she was gone.

Dr. Bernie S Siegel gives a lovely example in his book '365 Prescriptions for the Soul' by New World Library, of how spirit can make meaningful contact through butterflies and other animals.

"Prescription 41 Saying Goodbye

Many years ago, a patient of mine went to the Hawaiian island of Kauai to die. Her mother lived there, and my patient wanted to heal her relationship with her mother before she died.

Several years later I was invited to speak and present a workshop on the island. One day my wife and I entered a store and noticed a tiger swallowtail butterfly trapped in a large chandelier. My wife felt the need to rescue it, and so she climbed on the counter and held her hand out to the butterfly, which flew onto her palm. Then she climbed down. We went outside to release it, but the butterfly wouldn't leave. My wife tried brushing it off of one shoulder, but it just flew to the other. So we stopped trying to brush it off and allowed it to accompany us.

That night I said 'Bobbie you need to let that butterfly go we'll crush it if we take it to bed with us.'

She went out on the porch, returned, and said `I brushed it off my shoulder'

I said `Honey, it's sitting on your other shoulder.' we finally arranged a plate of sweet water on a kitchen counter, and the butterfly settled on its rim for the evening.

The next day, the butterfly hopped on and went to the workshop with us. I put it in a paper bag and planned to use it as part of my talk about life as a series of beginnings, not endings. After discussing the symbolism of the caterpillar and the butterfly, I opened the bag and let out our butterfly to demonstrate. The butterfly spent the day overhead, and then left after the workshop.

Why did it spend so much time with us? My answer was that it represented the spirit and consciousness of my patient and was her way of thanking me and saying goodbye."

I think butterflies often act as spiritual messengers and had a large blue butterfly tattooed on my arm, where I can always see it, after watching the film `The Blue butterfly'. In the film which stars William Hurt, a young boy is cured of `terminal 'cancer after going in search of a rare blue butterfly. There is certainly a lot of magical energy about them.

I remember preparing for a surgical procedure by getting up extra early on the day of the operation to walk through a nearby forest area. I thought the beauty and tranquility of nature would calm my nerves. I was amazed to find, for the only time ever, that the whole forest was a carpet of butterflies and every step I took saw clouds of butterflies take to the air. It was a breathtakingly beautiful experience, and later that day my sister who lives on the other side of the world from me, asked;

"Did you get the butterflies we sent you?"

"Yes millions of them thank you!" I replied delighted to know that it was her who had sent them.

This is where we see the power of the human spirit before death as well as after, a power, which we tend to use very sparingly, compared to our great potential. Powers akin to telepathy or maybe spirits or angels act for us as intermediaries.

The following true story related to me by the wonderful Medium Helen `Henry' Hezzell, shows how protective and helpful a spirit presence can be, even if it is not one of our own spirit loved ones, but one attached to a house or other fixed location occupied during their physical lifetime.

"Katherine.

Eighteen years ago, my husband Steve and I were living in a small seaside town in Lincolnshire, England. We had a tiny flat above a noisy arcade and we were already feeling overcrowded with our young daughter Tamsin living with us and now I was heavily pregnant with our second daughter Shantika. We decided that it was time to buy a house and so we went out looking for one big enough for our growing family. Eventually we found a terraced house in a long street at the outskirts of the town. Our first impression was that it looked suitable and we were amazed to find that the inside seemed much larger than we expected. There were three bedrooms, a lounge, a dining room and a kitchen. As we entered the house for the first time we noticed a heaviness in the air in the hallway, and as we made our way upstairs. As we turned on to the upstairs landing I felt a sudden chill but as we made our way further along it became calmer. Steve and I walked in to the first bedroom, which was quiet, bright and overlooked the street, but as we came out of that room and made our way to the next bedroom I had the disconcerting feeling that somebody was watching me!

Despite these strange sensations and the apprehension that we both felt, we decided to buy the house and hoped that we were making the right decision.

When we moved in, Steve and I took the bright front bedroom and put Tamsin in the next room.

A few days later I felt very ill, the pregnancy hadn't gone well at all and Steve put me to bed and went downstairs to care for Tamsin. I felt really awful and was drifting in and out of consciousness, so I felt very relieved when I felt the bed go down and assumed Steve had come to sit with me but I was too tired to speak and drifted back to sleep. When I awoke later I was alone in the room so I just lay there for about half an hour and then Steve came in to see how I was feeling. I thanked him for sitting with me and taking care of me but he said he had been downstairs the whole time with Tamsin, watching the television and he hadn't been with me at all! I realized that someone from spirit had been there with me, watching over me.

A few months after giving birth to Shantika there were still strange inexplicable things happening in the house. We decided to move our two girls in to the front bedroom and we moved into the next room. We had made a few alterations, moving the bedroom door further along the landing corridor and we had placed a mirror belonging to my late grandmother 'Nana', on the landing wall in between the two bedrooms.

A few more months passed when early one morning before any of us were really awake; Tamsin came flying in to our bedroom to say Shantika was poorly. I rushed in and found her in her cot, motionless and blue, she had obviously suffered a convulsion and her eyes were rolled back in her head. The ambulance arrived and Steve went with Shantika to the hospital, she was diagnosed with meningitis and spent two frightening weeks in intensive care. Thank goodness Tamsin had raised the alarm or her sister might not have been here today. Luckily she made a full recovery and is now a healthy young woman with a child of her own. When we asked Tamsin what had happened, she said that a girl had shaken her awake to tell her that Shantika was ill. To us the spirit had performed a miracle that saved our baby's life and we were very grateful. By now we had come to refer to our spirit as Katherine, which was the name, she gave me during mediumship contact.

More months passed and strange things began happening with our electrical appliances, which is often a way that spirit makes itself known or attracts our attention, the radio would begin to play or the kettle would switch itself on, all sorts of things happened. I kept saying to Steve that it was Katherine trying to warn us that there was something wrong with the electricity. A few days later we received a phone call at work to say that there had been a fire at the house. The electric oven had caught fire but luckily the nanny and the children were safe with neighbors and the fire brigade was putting it under control. We knew that they had had a lucky escape and that Katherine had indeed been trying to warn us that something was wrong. From that day onwards the electrical spirit activity never happened again.

If you stood in our kitchen at night with the lights on and

the curtains open, you could sometimes sense or get a glimpse of Katherine in the window, but mainly we sensed her at the top of the stairs. We were not afraid of Katherine; she was just a lonely soul who hadn't been able to move on. I believe that she was about 15 years of age with a pretty face and long dark hair and was lonely and withdrawn. She wore long clothing and a white high-necked blouse. She gave me the impression that she had been kept prisoner in the upper part of the house during her last years on earth, until she could stand it no more and hung herself at the top of the stairs. We felt she liked our company as we always spoke to her and brought our children up to accept the presence of spirit. She enjoyed our family life, especially the children. When Shantika was around 15 months old and I was giving her a bath one day, she swung around and started laughing and chatting away, but she wasn't talking to me. She was talking whilst looking straight through me and then suddenly she started waving and saying bye bye. After that Shantika turned back around and started playing with her bath toys as though nothing had happened! I knew that Katherine had been laughing and playing with her; she loved our two little girls and always protected them from harm.

When we finally left that house to move 100 miles further north we were sure we glimpsed Katherine with tears in her eyes at the window, watching us leave. Katherine is one spirit person that my family and I will never forget, and I hope others that live in her house will feel as loved and protected as we did."

Helen's story is a good example of how spirit presence can be positive and even life saving, even if it isn't one of your own loved ones.

Distance healing is an example of the power of spirit both sides of the veil and the power of prayer has also been scientifically proven. Our spiritual powers to help one another are phenomenal. Sending healing to another can be easily achieved and even healing colors might be perceived by the recipient, if the sender focuses on this. Do not be afraid to ask to be added to prayer lists if you are finding your bereavement very difficult. People love to help in this way, and God will joyfully provide you with everything you need for your emotional and spiritual healing.

Your own spirit is also phenomenally powerful and you can tap into this during your meditations. Call upon the Holy Spirit within you, your own Divine spark to magnify and expand. During meditation imagine this Divine spark residing in your solar plexus area or your solar plexus chakra, and then during deep breathing imagine the light expanding to fill your whole body with Holy light. Fill your aura as well with this beautiful healing light and feel yourself glowing with well being and strength. Try an affirmation such as:

> "I am filled with Divine light and I feel the love of spirit all around me. I am never alone; for my angels and my spirit loved ones guide me every step of the way."

You are never alone no matter how lonely you may feel, you always have your own holy spirit within, the love of God and the angels and the support of your guardian angels and spirit loved ones.

Remember you are always safe.

CHAPTER 9

LOSING A CHILD

It is often considered that losing a child is the most painful of losses, and certainly those of us who are parents know how deeply bonded we are to our children. No parent should have to bear the loss of a child at any age; it feels as though it goes against nature. Yet one in three pregnancies in the western world end in natural miscarriages and many more parents suffer the unimaginable trauma of cot deaths, accidents and terminal childhood illnesses. Even losing an adult child can be indescribably painful, because to us they are always our children.

Although I lost two of my babies to miscarriage, I do not pretend to begin to understand the pain of losing a baby that has been delivered full term or lived to be a toddler or a teenager; the anguish of this is especially hard to bear. Fortunately there are some very good support groups available, and meeting with other bereaved parents may help.

Doreen lost one of her daughters at an adult age but mentally

Angela was always a child. She cites the following anonymous poem as having helped her to cope with her grief it speaks of how God lends us our children:

"I will lend you for a time a child of mine," he said
For you to love while she lives, and mourn for when she's dead.
It may be six or seven years or twenty-two or three
But will you till I call her back, take care of her for me?
She'll bring her charms to gladden you, and should her stay be brief,
You'll have her lovely memories, as solace for your grief.
I cannot promise that she'll stay, since all from earth return...
But there are lessons taught down there, I want this child to learn.
I've looked the wide world over in search of teachers true,
And from the throngs that crowd life's lanes, I have selected you.
Now will you give her all your love,
Nor think the labor vain...
Nor hate me when I come to call her back again?
I fancied that I heard them say:
`Dear Lord thy will be done!
For all the joys Thy child shall bring, the risk of grief we'll run.
We'll shelter her with tenderness, we'll love her while we may,
And for the happiness we've known, forever grateful stay.
But should the angels call for her,
Much sooner than we've planned,
We'll brave the bitter grief that comes and try to understand'."

In reality of course the understanding part, is a lifelong challenge and we may never truly understand the physical separation caused by death at any age, but with luck we will feel assured that our babies and children spirit side are always with us and are cared for by God the angels and our other spirit loved ones.

Doreen's experience of losing a baby minutes after the birth were quite different. In those days, the 1970's, this sort of neonatal death and stillbirths were handled very insensitively.

Doreen was told not to even look at her baby as it was whisked away from her. Later when she asked to bury Nicola and have a funeral for her she was told it was too late; her body had already been disposed of in someone else's coffin! This seems incredibly crass to us these days, when parents are now encouraged to spend time with their dead baby and take photographs, footprints and so on and are given the opportunity to give them a proper funeral ceremony. But in those days there was no support system whatsoever and Doreen was soon told by her doctor that she really ought to be over it by now! I was also given this advice two weeks after miscarrying a much wanted baby. Really health professionals ought to have more training and sensitivity in this area. Doreen remembers crying for months after losing Nicola at birth and 21 years later she was still very much on her mind as she bought a bonsai tree to honor her 21st birthday, (the tree was about the same age.) Planting a tree, naming a lost baby that never went to term and including them in the family tree are all things, which might help a grieving parent. I placed homemade certificates to remember my girls Rose and Holly, in amongst our family folder of birth certificates and planted a Rose bush and a Holly tree in their honor. These small gestures helped me feel that their existence however brief was being recognized as I felt so many people, including my husband, would rather sweep the whole issue under the carpet and never speak of it again. I however felt moved to help others who had experienced such a loss and in the spirit of making it count I appealed for poems relating to the subject, which I felt, might help others. A book on all aspects of the joy and pain of motherhood was planned, but to date it has yet to be published, and so I will share some of the poetry and accounts with you in a moment.

Some find keeping a journal or an open letter to the child can be healing and others find that writing poetry can help. Here are some poems expressing the loss of a child written by ordinary people who do not necessarily normally think of themselves as poets. Many of these poems are shared with the hope of helping others to cope with similar losses and were shared with me some years ago.

"Picture in my Heart by Cheryl Anderson
Giving birth to you was an experience, the pain I soon forgot,
As I lay in my bed just watching you sleeping in your cot.
Your beautiful little features so perfect in every way,
I prayed to God to thank Him each and every day.
The weeks that passed were wonderful; you grew so strong and aware,
I knew that you were contented; I could feel you knew I cared.
I never smoked in pregnancy: you were a smoke-free zone,
And I did everything possible to give you a loving home.
But then one night I checked on you, I knew something wasn´t right,
You looked a funny color; I just hoped it was the light.
My heart was racing; my head in a whirl, my hands began to shake,
I scooped you up in to my arms, praying that you would wake.
But your body was cold and floppy; your breathing was no more,
And your eyes did not open, as the light shone through your door.
When the Doctor arrived, his head hung low; no words needed to be said,
I knew that God had taken you; I knew that you were dead.
A `classic case of cot death´, the coroner said to me,
But the guilt and pain were unbearable; was this true reality?
In the days that followed, my heart now broken in two,
I found no point in anything; I just wanted to be with you.
When the day came for your funeral, your coffin so very small,
The memories of your tiny face were all I could recall.
I wiped the tears of sadness; my heart sank very low,
And why God had to take you, I will never know.
But summers have come, and winters have passed, it's now been

many years,
But that has not stopped me thinking of you and crying many tears.
Motherhood did not last for long, before we had to part,
But you are always in my thoughts little one
And your picture is in my heart."

This poem illustrates how ridiculous it is to expect someone to be over a loss in a short time. Love is forever and healing from that loss may take many years or a whole lifetime. Healing happens when we know our loved ones are still with us spiritually, and that we can see them in our dreams and hold them in our arms. But the pain of physical separation and the feeling of having been robbed of years together on the physical plain is one of life's greatest challenges. Whether we feel grief stricken, or feel we are beginning to heal and move on, all feelings are natural and appropriate at the time. Grieving and healing take time.

Janet Corcoran captures the sense of grief and the feeling of being robbed of time together, in the following poem she wrote after her young son Alex was run over and killed by a very elderly man with poor eyesight.

"Alex: our Joy"
by Janet Corcoran.
I thought I knew what grief was,
What a fool: I knew nothing at all.
All those pains of yesterday were nothing compared to this;
Helplessness, loss of belief in anything good,
All consuming, tearing pain,
Never again to walk in the sun,
Never again to smile properly,
Never again to feel peace,
Never again to feel happiness,
Always a hole, always pain, always hatred.
I see you everywhere, a constant reminder,

Of all those conversations that we are never going to have, all those occasions we are not going to share.
I remember the exact shade of your eyes,
The shape of your ears, your freckles and your golden hair,
The turn of your head and mischievous smile,
And every minute of every day I ask why? Why? Why?"

The experience Janet has of seeing her son everywhere is one of spirits abilities to say hello, they might quite literally transpose their face on to that of another person, or make sure that somebody who strongly resembles them sits near you in the hospital, or on the bus, or in the theatre. And we should never doubt that our spirit loved ones *are with us* at important occasions such as births, weddings and christenings, birthday parties and even funerals. We are never truly separated no matter how much pain we feel at those lost years and the agony of what might have been. When you come to believe that your loved one can still listen to you, comfort you and guide you, you may feel some relief.

I can strongly identify with Janet's description of all consuming, tearing pain as I well remember feeling as though Peter's soul was literally being ripped apart from mine. The pain was unbearable. I also remember praying to God to let me understand why he had to suffer and die. At first I began with:

"Why did he have to suffer for a whole week? Why did he pass in such a ghastly manner?"

And although God never gave me a satisfactory answer `why', he did help me to gradually rephrase the questions, until I began to be able to put a positive spin on my prayers, which gradually transformed into:

"Thank God he only suffered for a week, and thank God that I could be with him at the end."

I have given up asking why? It is one of the unknowable mysteries of life that we can only heal with the faith that everyone passes at their perfect time, or that everything happens for a reason. Remember that we are all walking to God and we will all arrive at the perfect time for us, no matter how painful it is for those that we have temporarily left behind.

For those who are open to contact from their loved ones there is always the hope that they will somehow let us know that they are safe and well spirit side, and that they still watch over us.

Audrey K Price expresses how she senses that she is only separated from her child by a veil that keeps us from view after this life; and she clings to the hope and belief, that she is near and will be there for her, when her time comes to pass to spirit.

"Child of my heart
Child of my heart we had to part,
Many years have passed by
And I have stopped asking why
You were taken from me.
Child of my heart, my love spans the years,
You're close to me now that I've stopped shedding tears.
My heart feels so warm when I think of you;
For its only a veil that hides you from view.
Child of my heart, when I end my long day
I hope you'll be there to lighten my way."

Many parents are lucky enough to experience their children return to them as visions, feelings or even sense them creep into bed for a cuddle. I have been very blessed to experience this with my two baby girls as you know. Kath Taylor, who was unfortunate enough to lose her mother and her baby within 3 days of one another, provided me with this anonymous poem:

"In a baby castle, just beyond my eye
My baby plays with angel toys that money cannot buy.
Who am I to wish him back into this world of strife?
No; play on my baby, you have eternal life.
At night when all is quiet and when sleep forsakes my eyes
I'll hear his tiny footsteps come running to my side
His little hands caress me, so tenderly and sweet.
I breathe a prayer and close my eyes and embrace him in my sleep.
Now I have a treasure that I rate above all others:
I have known true glory and I am still his mother."

This simple poem describes beautifully the joy of embracing a spirit child and also answers an important question that often arises when a parent loses their only child: am I still a parent? The answer of course is a strong yes and you always will be.

I have had many poems from parents who have lost older children to drowning accidents and traffic accidents and I have been amazed at how time has helped them to look back and smile, when it would be so easy to look back and cry. Looking back at memories and deciding to smile at them instead of letting them overwhelm you with grief is a great step forward when you can make it and it works for losses of all ages and kinds. Nearly three years on from the loss of my husband, the family can now talk openly about the good times and laugh again at the fun we had and the silly things and jokes that happen within family life. This is a huge gift and keeps the memory of the person alive in a very important and special way. It seems they are more with you than ever when you can look back and smile. They rejoice with you because they do not enjoy seeing you sad and want you to know that they are right there beside you, through good times and bad.

Some feel happiness can only be restored when we are

reunited in death, but hopefully as time begins its healing process spirit will give us moments of true happiness right now.

It is very important to remember that no matter what the circumstances were, that surrounded your loved one's time to pass, you have the right to feel happy again as soon as you are ready. It can be particularly hard not to feel guilty if you have prayed long and hard that God would take your loved one, because they were suffering so terribly. I spent days praying for a happy release for my grandfather when he was very seriously ill in 1974 and I was just eleven years old. I felt guilty for years after he passed that I had somehow `caused' his death with my prayers. A child cannot appreciate the great release from pain that has manifested and may feel only remorse. When my husband was desperately ill and could no longer walk, talk, see or eat it was just a question of time until he passed and I was amazed to find myself once more praying to God that he take my most beloved to heaven and free him from this life of pain and anguish. Days passed and I prayed more and more, but even so when God finally let him pass I felt a mixture of relief, grief and anger at God for making this happen. The reason for sharing this with you is to reassure you that all emotions and feelings are acceptable and normal including, relief and happiness should they be part of the picture.

Valerie Trevallion watched her severely disabled daughter suffer all through her life, and then suddenly received a phone call to say that the hospital had made a mistake with her medication and she had died suddenly at the age of 8. After the initial grieving and shock, Valerie couldn't help but feel relieved for her daughter, who she knew would suffer no more and she wrote this poem to try and explain her mixed emotions:

"Ana's Freedom
It would be wrong to say I'm happy
Wrong to say I'm glad

It would be right to say I'm sorry
Right to say I'm sad
But what is right and wrong?
For they are only words
And it would be wrong to say I'm sorry
If really I am glad
You'd want me to be happy
Want me to be glad;
So why should I say I'm sorry
If I cannot feel sad?
Now we both are happy
And now we both are glad
That you have found your freedom
And no longer need be sad."

I think Valerie was very brave in her attitude and unselfish because she realized that her daughter would be happier, freer and more able in spirit and was happy for her.

It is also very brave to allow yourself to feel happy if that is what comes to you. No feeling is ever wrong, they are feelings. Feelings come from your thoughts so if you are feeling very bad that is a sign from your body that you are thinking negative or unhappy thoughts. Try to replace your sadness, guilt, loneliness or unhappiness with a positive thought about the future, the nature of eternal life or a happy memory and your feelings will change. Your emotions are feedback telling you whether you are on the right path. Turning emotions and feelings around during the grieving process can be extremely challenging but it *can be done.* This is not to suggest that you force yourself to put on a brave face for others whilst denying your own pain because that can lead to its own problems. But do try and be happy as often as you can, your spirit loved one will be delighted. Valerie is also wise and strong in realizing that new love can bring comfort and is no disloyalty to those who have passed. She was blessed to go on and have 3 more children after the loss of her daughter Aria, and she wrote this to describe her new happiness.

"What is life if not for living?
What is love if not for giving?
What are tears if not for shedding?
What is fear if not for dreading?
What is pain if not for feeling?
What is time if not for healing?
What are words if not for saying?
What is hope if not for praying?
And yet my life is lost
My love is dead
My tears are dry
My fears are none
My pain is numb
My time is short
My words are few
My hope is gone
I exist in a world where one survives
On memories, secrets, deaths and lies...
But then that cry from within the cot
Awakened my senses and I reviewed my lot!
From that moment I looked not back
But forward to a better track;
Where life is worth living
Where love is worth winning
Where tears are worth saving
And fear is worth sharing
Where pain is worth bearing
Where time is worth having
Where words are worth meaning
And hope is worth knowing.
Therefore my thanks to that baby so small

So helpless and pure
Wrapped up in her shawl
Who gave me new life, new meaning, new hope
A life now worth living, with a far wider scope."

It is not always possible to have another child after a loss, but it can bring great joy and a sense of completeness if you allow love guiltlessly back into your heart and never compare the second child to the one that you have lost. Similarly losing a beloved partner or spouse may leave you feeling that you will never love again and certainly never remarry, but God and your guardian angels and spirit loved ones may have other plans further down your life's path, so keep your heart open.

My late husband never felt he would remarry when he lost his first wife to cancer, but a few years later there we were married and his life took on new meaning again. He never stopped loving his first wife and she was doubtlessly watching over us, but we never allowed that to come between us. There is always room for loving spirit.

Flo Mathias was devastated when she lost her son John soon after his birth in 1964 and her first feelings were that she would never know happiness again until they were reunited in death, as her following poem shows, but an event two years later made her realize that he was still with her.

"John
You grew inside my body; I planned for you each day.
I waited for you patiently and dreamed about the way
I would hold you in my arms and cry the tears of joy,
Instead, my tears were tears of sorrow for you, my baby boy.
I never held you to my breast; I only saw your face
Then you were taken from me and laid in your resting place.
The pain will stay forever, deep inside my heart,
The anguish of that day tore my world apart.

In time, when I leave this earthly place we will meet again,
Then I will cry the tears of joy instead of tears of pain."

Happily Flo was then given the most wonderful gift as she relates in the following account:

> "One day, two years after John had died; I was busy doing my ironing. I was about to carry a pile of clean clothes upstairs when something made me look up. Standing at the top of the stairs was a toddler in a long white gown. The baby looked at me and smiled. I rushed towards the child but there was no one there. Was it my baby letting me know he is happy? I like to think so. I want to think so."

I don't think there is any doubt that this beautiful spirit child was her son making contact, and I pray that every parent who has lost a child will be blessed by such a visit.

To encourage a baby or young child to visit simply close your eyes in a relaxed sate and invite them into your arms and your dreams, and hopefully you will feel them snuggle close to you, or see them in your dreams. Never be afraid of spirit contact from your loved ones and remember that love and fear cannot coexist.

CHAPTER 10

MAKING IT COUNT

It may not happen right away, but sooner or later you may feel inspired to turn your loss into something positive, in tribute to your loved one, and for the sake of others.

Lance Armstrong, the celebrated cycling champion, expressed this spirit after his miraculous recovery from stage four cancer. He wanted to make something positive out of one of the most traumatic events in his life, he felt almost a responsibility as a cancer survivor, to help and inspire others. This remarkable man even came to see his cancer as something very positive, as it had taught him so many valuable lessons and he now understood so much more about life. He fought back to win the Tour De France, one of the most grueling physical challenges in sport today. Lance now helps others through The Lance Armstrong Foundation and through his truly inspirational books such as 'It's not about the bike.'

Now I am not suggesting that every bereaved person will feel like tackling something as challenging as winning a championship title, or that we should all feel obliged to do something in tribute to our loved ones, but many *do* and they find it one of the best and most meaningful therapies that there is.

When I lost my husband I felt inspired to help others through writing this spiritually inspired guide to bereavement. I felt that I had so much to share and had learned so much that might support and help others, that writing this book seemed the logical way to make sense of my loss. Often we face a challenge in life and then feel that perhaps we were picked for this experience in order to help others, or to campaign to improve a situation. Often a parent or relative of a murdered child has turned this most painful of losses into something positive, by campaigning to make sure that everything is being done, to prevent more child murders. Think of the parents of Sarah Payne for example, who campaigned to improve the law regarding pedophiles in the UK in order to protect other parents and children from suffering such a horrendous tragedy.

Others do something as simple as ask for donations to be sent to a hospice, or a cancer or other research charity, instead of having the traditional funeral wreaths. Or the dying person themselves may have willed such a gift or the setting up of a fund or foundation to help others.

You should not feel guilty if you do not get this type of inspiration; it is just one of many ways that we pay tribute to the lives of our loved ones in spirit. Getting up each morning and carrying on with life is a tribute in itself, if you are feeling like hiding from the world or giving up, but sooner or later you may feel inspired to do something more.

'Making it count' is a win: win situation because as you help others, you will be helping yourself to heal and live on in a more fulfilling and happy manner.

Let me explain better by giving you another example:

In 2002 Doreen lost her daughter to a long fight with a terminal illness. The trauma of this is difficult to explain and Doreen had been caring for her daughter through an illness which caused crippling pain and degeneration over a period of more than twenty years. When her daughter passed to spirit, she left a huge gap in her parents′ lives. Suddenly their main twenty four hour focus of love and attention had slipped away. Doreen and her husband and family were devastated. It all seemed so unfair, but over the years of caring for a severely ill child, they had accumulated a huge amount of experience and understanding. In tribute to her daughter who constantly made her presence from spirit amply clear, Doreen signed up to undertake a course which would qualify her as a counselor. She felt the need to turn her experiences of such a great loss into a gift to others. The course was challenging and Doreen had been away from the world of paid work and study for more than thirty years, but during each year of the course she was awarded the prize for best student. The awards and praise kept coming and her work is now a huge support to all her clients, as she now works as a counselor and is able to share so much love and understanding. She is a source of joy and sunshine to all she meets and credits a lot of her survival skills to the strength she gains, from an almost indestructible sense of humor. I am sure that her daughter is very pleased to see her mother spreading so much happiness, reassurance and skilled advice.

Doreen explains how she came to decide to become a counselor:

"After losing Angela I felt so empty, I had not only lost my daughter but also my job as her twenty four hour carer. She had been the focus of our lives for so long and I did not know where to begin to rebuild my life. Yet I feel Angela guided me completely from spirit. About a year after her passing, I was at the local supermarket one morning feeling so bereft and

wondering what to do with my life, when suddenly a leaflet fell on to the conveyor belt about a local counseling course, and I felt guided to pick it up. I could feel Angela urging me to take the leaflet home and study it, so I did. The course sounded perfect for me and I signed up for it. Counseling has really changed my life and given it a new focus. I feel I can help others because of my own experiences and I also feel it is a tribute to Angela. I found grief very isolating but Angela guided me back into the world of the living. She also helped me move on by visiting me in my dreams. In one particularly vivid dream I saw her reflected in a mirror, just as she was when she died, but as I kept looking she became younger and younger until she was a baby again. Then she spoke to me:
'I can do everything now Mum, I am fine and you have to let me go.'

It was hard but I knew she was right and felt much more at peace after this visit. She has given me the strength and support I need from spirit to make a difference to others. I will always love her and miss her but I know she is much happier spirit side and no longer in pain and she is with me always. She helps me with my counseling; I couldn't have done it without her."

Doreen really made it count, and she has recently been asked to teach new students which will spread even more comfort and happiness into the world. We can all make a difference.

I feel fairly certain that if the idea of 'making it count' appeals to you, you will already have an inspired idea of how you would like to do this. But here are some more ideas that might help if you are undecided where to begin. Depending on the lifetime interests of your loved one, or the cause of their death, you may decide to do one of the following:

- Raise money for a cancer research charity.
- Raise money for a cancer support charity.
- Join a support group for cancer sufferers and their families.
- Establish a support group if none exists in your area.
- Support people undergoing loss and bereavement through friendship and understanding.
- Campaign to raise awareness about prevention, detection and treatment of the particular illness involved.
- Volunteer to work for a charity or in a charity shop which raise funds for the health area concerned.
- Start a charity in honor of the person that will benefit others in meaningful ways (take legal advice on this.)
- Raise awareness about the perils of drunken driving, drug abuse, unprotected sex or other relevant danger depending on the cause of death.
- Help in a children's charity, older persons support centre, hospice or become a hospital visitor.
- Join a society that helps people come to term with cot death and other childhood tragedies.
- Join a prayer group or healing circle.

- Write a book in tribute to your loved one, either for wide circulation or to share between friends and family.
- Campaign for new laws that would prevent a tragedy such as a child murder or racially motivated killing.
- Learn a new skill such as counseling, teaching, healing or nursing.
- Smile at strangers and brighten their day, take time to be thoughtful and helpful every day.
- Join campaigns for world peace, love and harmony, if war or hatred were implicated in your loved ones passing.
- Continue their life's work in some way if this is relevant.
- Plant a tree or garden in their memory.
- Sponsor a bench in a beautiful or meaningful location, upon which others can sit and take in the view.

I am sure you can think of many more ways to make a positive contribution to the world that you might never have done if it wasn't for your loss.

As we give we receive, and as we teach we learn and enrich our own lives. It is said that a teacher teaches what he or she needs to learn; just as it is also said that when a student is ready the teacher will appear.

How many magical 'coincidences' and synchronicities do we need to experience in a lifetime before we accept the probability [illegible] these are no coincidence? More likely they are God moving [illegible]sterious ways, or angels or spirit giving us a push in the right direction. Having faith that everything occurs for a reason may help you at many times in your life, even though the cruel sadness of the loss of a loved one may challenge this belief to the extreme. If you are open to the possibility, I am sure that the right people, situations, books and other gifts will literally manifest in your path.

In the beginning you will most likely be on the receiving end of these gifts of wisdom, revelation or comfort either directly from spirit or through new friends and resources that seem to magically appear in your life. As time moves along and you begin to heal from your grief, you may find yourself offering the gift of love and support to another bereaved or challenged person. The gift of your experience and the deep wisdom you gain as you travel the healing road will enable you to be a great source of guidance and comfort to others. Your mere survival from such a traumatic life event will inspire hope and admiration. Your loss may even begin to make more sense to you, as you are able to discuss it and how to cope with others who find themselves on a different part of life's journey.

I clearly remember my mother sitting on the end of my bed shortly after my first miscarriage. I felt devastated. She amazed me by telling me that for the past thirty years she had wondered why she herself had had to suffer the trauma of miscarriage and now at last, it made sense to her. It was in her eyes, a gift that she was able to reach out and touch my heart now with the genuine knowledge that she really did understand what I was going through. In that moment it made sense to her. Her loss was a gift of understanding. I should say that at that time in 1992 I thought she was crazy to feel that way but nearly twenty years later I realize how right she was.

We are all walking a journey, some further ahead than others; some gaining expertise of the landscape that will help those who follow, others needing a helping hand. At various stages of our life we will find ourselves on different parts of the journey. Some parts are a pleasurable walk through meadows on a sunny day; other parts seem like climbing Mount Everest without the necessary experience or equipment. Along the way we may experience the help of angels in the form of earthly friends or literally from an invisible angelic force. Or equally if we are lucky, we may have the chance to give that same selfless support to another. Sometimes a simple smile or well-timed hug will do the trick, but often it will be a longer slower process of support through inspiration, sympathy or example. Every time that you extend your hand to help another based on your own experience of grief or trouble, you are making your loss and the life of your loved one count in a very special way.

If this is through campaigning, supporting or sharing, writing, counseling or simply listening and caring or praying, you will be giving back a great gift to the world. At the time of reading this book, this may feel far from your mind, or you may already be following or thinking of this course of action, it is my hope that you will keep this book by your side and dip into its chapters during the first two to three years of your recovery and adjustment, because the various stages we pass through are so many and varied. Many of you will already have found some books unhelpful in the extreme and literally thrown them across the room or destroyed them. Hopefully you have also been guided to other books and sources of comfort that have touched notes and places within your soul that resonate with meaning and enrich your healing process.

Whether we choose to see life as a circle or a continuing journey we will all find ourselves facing challenges and how we respond dictates how we feel.

It is true that many people feel that you do not `get over' a bereavement or other tragedy, and that you simply learn to live with it. I would like to think that there is enough spiritual ice and angelic and spiritual support here, for us, that we to a point where we really can believe that our loved ones stay at our sides eternally, and that the physical separation, is to a large extent an illusion. We can continue to have dream visits, spiritual contact and support from our loved ones for as long as we need it.

When we lose a loved one it is easy to feel angry with God or to stop believing in him altogether. You might feel confused and need to understand how this could happen to someone so special to you. You may feel victimized by God if a series of unfortunate events occur in your life, but I truly hope that your faith will be returned to you.

I am not speaking of any particular religious denomination or set of beliefs, but rather of one's personal faith in something, which unites us all. God may be seen as described in the Christian bible or as seen by many other faiths, but equally you may think of him or her, as the universal love and spirit energy that unites us all. Choosing whatever image is meaningful to you can help you feel that you are never alone. A little of God , the Holy spirit, the life force source energy is within us all and basically is what makes up our individuality and our soul: the part that can never be destroyed and lives for all eternity. We are all made of Divine source energy. We are all walking towards God, as described in the following lesson from A Course in Miracles:

> Lesson 155
> "We walk to God. Pause and reflect on this. Could any way be holier, or more deserving of your effort, of your love and full intent? What way could give you more than everything... we walk to God."

The thought suggested accompanying this lesson being:

> "I will step back and let Him lead the way.
> For I would walk along the road to Him."

I remember a turning point in my own journey through grief came around five months after my loss when I realized that howling like a banshee and clutching an urn of my husband's ashes, really wasn't achieving very much. Obviously it was supremely important for my mental and physical health at the time, that I had this outlet for my grief, but I came to realize that I was walking each day one day further from his passing to spirit and one day closer to my own inevitable time to pass. The time was coming in which I would have to re evaluate how I was coping and where I would be going from that point onwards. The time for daily howling had come to an end. I needed to find other ways to heal and so will you.

Converting grief further along our journey into something that has strengthened us, is very important for healthy survival. The old saying by Frederich Nietzsche that what doesn't kill us, makes us stronger, is true to a large extent if we can move positively on with our journey. My son Daniel recently helped me to deal with physical pain by telling me that a hero of his from the world of basketball, Ganon Baker, inspired players by telling them that pain is weakness leaving the body. A sentiment, which follows naturally on from the idea that what does not kill us, makes us stronger.

You can adapt this U S Marines slogan to fit your spiritual and emotional pain during early grieving. If physical pain is weakness leaving the body, how could we make an emotional equivalent? Maybe tears are grief and suffering leaving the body? It certainly feels that if a million tears need to be shed, in order to heal, that they will be shed either all at once, or be stored up to be let out over a much longer period of time. Or that sadness or resentment unexpressed might show up later as physical suffering within the body. It is not unusual for a grieving person to feel all sorts of physical aches and pains as the grief and crying ing to be controlled or suppressed. The best answer to this pain is to let the floodgates of tears open if you can. Or follow up with some physical outlets for anger and resentment such as physical exercise or beating up cushions or a mattress with a strong walking stick.

You may at this moment, feel a long way from helping others through grief and other life challenges but I believe that day will come; if you are open to being healed and to healing.

I am not suggesting in this chapter that you become self-sacrificing and ignore your own needs. That would be a disaster to your own physical and mental well being. Indeed you need to learn to be gentler with yourself and learn the almighty power of the word 'NO'. But you may find comfort at some point in your journey from extending love and support to others.

Joel Rothschild in his book `Signals,' by Bantam Books does a terrific job of making the most painful loss of his best friend count in a big way. The book begins with Rothschild being skeptical about the afterlife, but a pact he makes with a friend soon changes this. His friend Albert persuades him that whoever reaches spirit first should try to signal the other one to prove the existence of life after life. This true story is well worth reading as it shows how Albert managed to signal to his friend over and over again that he is still around him in spirit. Continually sending him hummingbirds in almost impossible places as well as beginning to speak to his friend and act as a spirit guide, Albert's determination to stay in touch is remarkable. Rothschild eventually develops the skills of a medium as a result of Albert's contact and he begins to bring messages through from other spirits for other people. Joel Rothschild's mediumship brings comfort to others in the midst of his own suffering, as many of his friends are dying from AIDS. The story is amazing and moving and written in a very genuine style. I would thoroughly recommend this book to you if you are in any doubt of the ability of spirit to stay in touch and keep watch over us. Joel moves from skeptic to believer and describes his evolving beliefs towards the end of his book:

"I believe that each and every one of us has the ability to communicate with deceased loved ones. I believe drugs, alcohol, caffeine, stress and other distractions from this existence inhibit that ability. When we are in a relaxed state, similar to a peaceful awakening from sleep or coming out of meditation, all of us can connect with our departed loved ones. They are always listening. They can and will answer us. Their voices can be very quiet. Rather than seeking validation from outside sources, we have to believe and trust in the love we have already shared. All of the messages and signals from Albert...were of an intimate and serious nature...and I have acquired a profound belief that, as Albert's final message to me relayed

`All of life's moments have meaning and purpose and are connected to a greater good.'

This keeps me from making quick judgments. Things are not always as they appear. Suffering and pain today may bring vast beneficial changes tomorrow.

I now believe our species is evolving in a positive direction. I believe we are slowly moving toward a `collective consciousness.' I believe most human beings are inherently good. I believe each and every one of us can effect positive change in the universe, and we effect that change by even the smallest act of kindness."

Joel's friendship beyond physical death with his friend Albert is a perfect example of how spirit stays with us, guides us and contacts us in so many ways. Albert also managed to help Joel develop a loving belief system even though he was going through a very challenging time and endured a lot of physical and emotional suffering. Joel found the strength to become the world's longest surviving AIDS patient and he has made it count [illegible]h his inspirational writing and the acts of kindness he uses [illegible]e a positive ripple effect in our world.

We can all make it count in our own way, for many of us it will be a catalyst for huge amount of spiritual development that we may be able to use to help ourselves and others.

Susan Elliott told me how she was affected by the death of her beloved son Darryl in a car accident. She wrote this account two years after her loss.

"My son Darryl was killed in a car crash two years ago, I have learnt a lot from this tragedy in many ways. I am a much better person now and I want to love and help people in all different ways. On reflection I had always helped people but when this tragedy occurred I asked myself the question `why am I here? ´ I now know what I have to do with my life even though at first I did not even want to live without Darryl. It's been a long, hard road and nothing has changed except that I have learned to live each day as it comes and try to cope. When I was seconds from suicide with grief I knew I needed help but not from a counselor so I prayed for Darryl to help me.

Soon afterwards, I was trying to vacuum my home when something kept telling me to go out for a walk and that is when my life changed. I went out and was drawn to a leaflet for no reason at all, saying `Keven Wade a medium´ was coming to our village hall. I felt I was being told to attend the event and so I went along. Keven came over to me straight away and told me in great detail everything that I had been through losing my son and then Darryl came through to prove that he is still alive, only his body has died, life is eternal and spirit lives on. He said it was like shedding your overcoat! I have been on a high ever since and have experienced a lot of wonderful contacts from Darryl and all my other loved ones in spirit. Like anything else in life you can fully understand it when it happens to you personally. Everything made sense and I felt so much happier knowing Darryl was always with me.

I am proud to say that I am now a Spiritualist and because of this I have learned to give spiritual healing to others. I am also training to be a spiritualist medium so that I will be able to help others have contact from their spirit loved ones.

Reflecting back now, I know that this tragedy had to happen to our son; it was his time to pass. The night of his cremation he woke me up to show me a vision of rebirth and happiness, which bought me comfort, and now I understand that he is always with me. Without his support from spirit I wouldn't be here writing this to you now.

I have had some beautiful dream visits from Darryl and he has taught me that we have so much to learn here on this earthly plane.

I am very proud of Darryl as he does a lot of good work supporting people still in this life and also works hard in spirit. I have learned that when a young child passes over to spirit he looks after them and explains that they have `come home.' He has also inspired me to help others through my spiritualist work."

Susan really has turned her loss into something positive and I am sure her healing and mediumship will make a real difference to all she helps. She really has made it count and along the way has developed a lot herself spiritually.

Remember we are all walking to God; we are all walking the same journey. We may take different paths, we may stumble occasionally, get lost or even seem to reach our destination too soon, but we are one, and we walk together.

I would like to end this chapter with a poem that has inspired millions and is particularly meaningful when you feel you might be walking alone:

FOOTPRINTS IN THE SAND
One night I dreamed I was walking along the beach with the Lord.
Many scenes from my life flashed across the sky.
In each scene I noticed footprints in the sand.
Sometimes there were two sets of footprints,
Other times there were only one set of footprints.
This bothered me because I noticed that during the low points of my life,
When I was suffering from anguish, sorrow or defeat,
I could see only one set of footprints.
So I said to the Lord,
"You promised me Lord,
That if I followed you,
You would walk with me always.
But I have noticed that during the most trying periods of my life
There have been only one set of footprints in the sand.
Why, when I needed you most, have you not been there for me?"
The Lord replied,
"The times when you have seen only one set of footprints in the sand,
Is when I carried you."

CONCLUSION

Hopefully now that you have read this book you will be finding comfort from the fact that your relationship with your loved one continues.

The relationship has changed only because the physical body has ceased to function, but death hasn't changed the most important aspects of your life together. Love and togetherness continue, your loved one continues at your side, guiding and loving you.

With luck you will have recognized and learned to be open to their continuing communication, whether it be directly to you or via a medium.

Spiritually you will be finding continual enlightenment as they guide and care for you.

Your relationship may have moved in to another dimension but it is as beautiful and important to you as it ever was.

Love and the human spirit are eternal; we need never feel truly alone. Spirit loves and surrounds us. Angels wait to help when we ask. God loves and cares for all of us and we are all walking home to Him.

If you have come to believe in reincarnation you will also

have the comfort of knowing that we will be with our loved ones again in many life times.

As time takes us further from their passing to spirit and nearer to our own passing we will be learning valuable lessons.

Life is a spiritual journey and love knows no end.

I sincerely hope that this book has helped with your healing.

Feel free to contact me if I can be of any further help.

One love

Deborah

Recommended Reading

Aromatherapy A guide for home use
Christine Westwood. Amberwood Publishing ltd
Angels 101
Doreen Virtue PH.D. Hay House INC
Healing with the Angels
Doreen Virtue PH.D. Hay House
Two Worlds as One A medium's life
Val Williams. Red Wing Publishing
I'm Grieving As Fast As I Can (How young widows and widowers can cope and heal)
Linda Feinberg. New Horizon Press
A Course in Miracles
Foundation for Inner Peace. Viking
Spirited
Tony Stockwell. Hodder Mobius
Embracing Eternity
Tony Stockwell. Hodder Mobius
Messages from the Masters (Tapping into the Power of Love)
Dr Brian Weiss. Piatkus
Don't Kiss Them Goodbye
Allison Dubois. Simon and Schuster
You Can Heal Your Life
Louise L. Hay. Hay House
Love Yourself, Heal Your Life Workbook
Louise L. Hay. Hay House
It's Not About the Bike
Lance Armstrong. Yellow Jersey Press
The Crystal Bible
Judy Hall. Godsfield Press

Recommended Listening

The Rose Garden

Val Williams.

Meet Your Loved Ones Meet Your Guides

Val Williams.

Mind Focus, an introduction to meditation

Tony Stockwell. IPMTV

Chakra Clearing

Doreen Virtue PH.D. Hay House Audio

Angel Therapy Meditations

Doreen Virtue PH.D. Hay House Audio

Past life Regression with the Angels

Doreen Virtue PH.D. Hay House Audio.

Contact with the author Deborah Kay Hayward

talks-with-angels@hotmail.com

www.talking-with-angels.com

To have a live mediumship or psychic reading with Deborah go to Liveperson at http://www.liveperson.com/talking-with-angels

Personally recommended UK mediums:

Val Williams val-williams57@hotmail.com

Karen Harris karison11@hotmail.com

Tom Harrison

Andrew de Vaal a.devaal@btopenworld.com

Peter Hind-Fletcher healer1@hotmail.co.uk

Ralph Keeton ralph@exorcisms.co.uk

Spain

Helen Henry Hezzell brucha59@hotmail.com

USA

Katherine Illescas illescas@yahoo.com